CCCC STUDIES IN WRITING & RHETORI

Edited by Victor Villanueva, Washington Sta

The   is to influence think about language in action and especially how writing gets taught at the college level. The methods of studies vary from the critical to historical to linguistic to ethnographic, and their authors draw on work in various fields that inform composition—including rhetoric, communication, education, discourse analysis, psychology, cultural studies, and literature. Their focuses are similarly diverse—ranging from individual writers and teachers, to work on classrooms and communities and curricula, to analyses of the social, political, and material contexts of writing and its teaching.

SWR was one of the first scholarly book series to focus on the teaching of writing. It was established in 1980 by the Conference on College Composition and Communication (CCCC) in order to promote research in the emerging field of writing studies. As our field has grown, the research sponsored by SWR has continued to articulate the commitment of CCCC to supporting the work of writing teachers as reflective practitioners and intellectuals.

We are eager to identify influential work in writing and rhetoric as it emerges. We thus ask authors to send us project proposals that clearly situate their work in the field and show how they aim to redirect our ongoing conversations about writing and its teaching. Proposals should include an overview of the project, a brief annotated table of contents, and a sample chapter. They should not exceed 10,000 words.

To submit a proposal, please register as an author at www.editorial manager.com/nctebp. Once registered, follow the steps to submit a proposal (be sure to choose SWR Book Proposal from the drop-down list of article submission types).

AFTER PEDAGOGY

THE EXPERIENCE OF TEACHING

Paul Lynch
Saint Louis University

Conference on College Composition and Communication

National Council of Teachers of English

"The Wanderer" by Antonio Machado, from *Selected Poems of Antonio Machado,* translated by Betty Jean Craige, copyright © 1978, reprinted by permission of Louisiana State University Press.

Staff Editor: Bonny Graham
Series Editor: Victor Villanueva
Interior Design: Mary Rohrer
Cover Design: Mary Rohrer and Lynn Weckhorst

NCTE Stock Number: 00875

Publication partially funded by a subvention grant from the Conference on College Composition and Communication of the National Council of Teachers of English.

Library of Congress Cataloging-in-Publication Data
Lynch, Paul, 1971-
   After pedagogy : the experience of teaching / Paul Lynch, Saint Louis University.
      pages cm. — (Studies in writing & rhetoric)
   Includes bibliographical references and index.
   ISBN 978-0-8141-0087-5 (pbk)
1. Composition (Language arts)—Study and teaching. I. Title.
   PN181.L96 2013
   808'.042071—dc23
                                                  2013036284

For Melody

Precept is less important than experience in almost every field.
—Quintilian, *Institutes of Oratory* (II.v.16)

CONTENTS

PROLOGUE: THE TUESDAY MORNING QUESTION

THIS PROJECT BEGINS WITH A QUESTION I hesitate to ask. I've imagined the question many times; I may have even muttered it once or twice at a conference or in a grad seminar. But I am still reluctant to enunciate it. Call it the "Monday Morning Question," the question that asks, "This theory (or idea, or philosophy) you're proposing is great and everything, but what am I supposed to do with it when the students show up on Monday morning?" Offered sometimes as a forthright engagement, sometimes as an intemperate challenge, sometimes as a cri de coeur, the Monday Morning Question is either the subtlest or the bluntest meeting of theory and practice in the work of composition. Asked well, the Monday Morning Question inspires inquiry. What are the practical implications of a theoretical awareness of one's pedagogy? How can and should pedagogies change when they are contextualized in their histories, histories from eras far different than our own? How should we respond when the reading we do away from the classroom undermines our assumptions about language and writing? But asked badly—asked, that is, in the way I have sometimes wanted to in my lesser moments—the Monday Morning Question can stifle inquiry by seeming to demand that any theoretical insight be justified with an immediate pedagogical application. Have some interpretation of a recondite philosopher? Discovered an obscure historical treatise on rhetoric? Found some troubling trend developing in the disciplinary literature? The skeptical manifestation of the Monday Morning Question can imply that such projects are relevant to composition only insofar as they directly shape classroom practice.

But whatever the spirit in which it is asked, the most troubling risk of the Monday Morning Question is the way it slots thought into the worn intellectual groove of theory-vs.-practice. This tired binary at once suggests two untenable ideas: either there is a nebulous and ephemeral thing called theory that cannot survive in the wilds of practice, or there is a rough-and-tumble realm called practice that will mar the pristine beauties of theory. This self-defeating choice has troubled composition for a long time. Twenty-five years ago, Louise Wetherbee Phelps described it in her book *Composition as a Human Science*. Regarding theory's entrance (or intrusion) into the pedagogical project of composition, Phelps observed that the field seemed to have reduced the issue to two bad options: "teachers could naively accept [theory] (along the lines of the banking model of education), or they could reject it as impractical, overly abstract, and irrelevant" (220). At its most extreme, this fracture has descended into recrimination, which Susan Jarratt describes: "Establishing 'composition' as a legitimate university field has entailed a heated defense of teachers as noble practitioners—front-line soldiers in the battle for literacy—as against ivory-tower literature scholars for whom teaching is secondary to theoretical or philosophic activities: i.e., scholarly research" (94). I do not mean to suggest that most, or even many, compositionists still think rigidly in either of these two ways. Rather, I mean to ask whether composition has finally sidestepped this division. For her part, Phelps offered *phronesis*, or practical wisdom, as a plausible workaround. Through a reading of Gadamer—along with Freire and Dewey—Phelps suggests that *phronesis* "makes it possible to address the previously unthinkable possibility that a discipline might constitute itself without submitting praxis to the domination of theory" (206). In resisting theory's domination, Phelps does not mean to reject it. Instead, her seemingly paradoxical position is that *phronesis* offers the best way for theory to enter into practice and to reshape it.

As persuasive as this argument is—and notwithstanding the wide influence of Freire and Dewey—it is less clear that Phelps's appeal to practical wisdom has resolved the theory–practice split. About a decade after Phelps published *Composition*, Gary Olson worried that the field was facing yet another round of "theory wars" that would pit theoretically informed scholarship against "straightforward" narratives of good teaching and good writing (both of which would be defined by accessibility for first-year students) ("Death").

This fight, according to Olson, was essentially a replay of the battles in the late 1980s, right around the time *Composition as a Human Science* appeared. Indeed, Olson comes to the same conclusion that Phelps had a decade before, going so far as to quote her observation that "deep in the disciplinary unconscious runs a strong undercurrent of anti-intellectual feeling that resists the dominance of theory in every institutional context of the field—journals, conferences, writing classrooms, textbooks, teacher education—and even in some forms of theory itself" (Phelps, qtd. in Olson, "Death" 24). That feeling, Olson argues, led some to dismiss theoretical inquiry as careerist maneuvering for disciplinary domination (29). While Olson rejects this reading of the field as a product of both strawman and ad hominem argument, he also welcomes a healthy and vigorous hegemonic struggle, one in which critical theory helps scholars to stretch composition's field of inquiry beyond its traditional bounds (30). Reminding his readers that "struggle can be collegial and congenial," he quotes Chantal Mouffe's distinction between enemies and adversaries and hopes that the latter term will characterize disagreement in rhetoric and composition (30).

Of course, Olson is right: just as we should reject the term *enemy* in favor of *adversary,* we should repudiate the idea that theoretical inquiry represents a betrayal of composition's true mission. But in avoiding this destructive distinction, Olson lays the foundations for another. His apologia for theory suggests that such scholarship will push the field beyond the classroom:

> Those who wanted to define the field *as one devoted not to just the teaching of writing* but to all aspects of how discourse works turned to critical theory from a wide variety of disciplines, including anthropology, feminist theory, philosophy, and sociology. Clearly, this latter group has made substantial progress. For twenty years, composition scholarship has developed as an interdisciplinary, "intellectual" enterprise—and we are much the richer because of it. (30; emphasis added)

In spite of all that I find right about this claim, what troubles me is the language suggesting that a focus on teaching is likely to retard the progress of composition's intellectual work. Certainly Olson's vision of agonism is salutary and necessary, but that vision also suggests something that Phelps tried to resist as much as composition's anti-intellectual tendencies—namely, that to accept the influence of theory is to move past pedagogy.

Let me be clear: I am not trying to position myself as Olson's adversary, much less his enemy. Much of the argument of the present work is premised on ideas that Olson has helped to articulate. But I am concerned about the ways in which those ideas are sometimes forwarded. Witness, for example, Sidney Dobrin's recent *Postcomposition*, which comes about ten years after Olson's prediction that the anti-intellectual pedagogues would end up starting a new round of theory wars. Yet if anyone is trying to start a war, it is Dobrin, who explicitly calls for a kind of "violence" against the discipline (113). Postcomposition, he writes, suggests a "creative destruction" of composition as a pedagogical enterprise (188). "Writing theory must move beyond composition studies' neurosis of pedagogy, must escape the shackles of classroom, students and management" (28). In addition to being neurotic, then, those interested in composition's teaching mission would also apparently enslave both the field and its students. It seems that the naïve expressivists are no longer the source of the fighting words.

While Dobrin offers the most extreme rejection of composition's traditional pedagogical mission, he is of course not the only scholar who would bristle at the Monday Morning Question. His work is only the latest contribution to "postpedagogy," whose basic claim is that composition can no longer be defined by pedagogy because pedagogy "hope," which has shaped the field for so long, is no longer available. After the Great Paradigm Shift from preprocess to process, the field has followed a series of smaller shifts until arriving at "postprocess," which is best defined not as a system of teaching but as an attitude about teaching. This attitude holds that teaching is too complex, too particular, too situated to be rendered in any repeatable and therefore portable way. Capital *P* Pedagogy, just like capital *T* Theory, guarantees nothing. Now we have moved beyond postprocess to postpedagogy, which tries to evade the pedagogical on the grounds that it is nearly impossible to speak about teaching without being tempted by the will-to-system, to process, and to pedagogy. Yes, runs this argument, we might encounter teachable moments, but no pedagogy can reliably occasion them. The best we can do is to create the conditions in which they might occur. Process cannot reliably result in product; the revelations of critical pedagogy do not bring about revolution. The stable self is not there to be expressed, and the construction of the social does not sufficiently account for struggle. There is, in short, no pedagogical solution to composition's troubled evolution. This is bound to be disorienting to a field that, for its first few decades at least, was defined by a search for a viable pedagogy.

To be sure, anyone who has taught for any length of time already knows that pedagogy does not often survive contact with the classroom. But now our theoretical inquiry has arrived at the same conclusion, a conclusion that demands our attention. And while Dobrin may stand alone in his call for violence, he is joined by a host of others in his desire to give up composition's pedagogical quest. In addition to Olson, we can find the postpedagogical idea expressed in the work of Diane Davis, Byron Hawk, Cynthia Haynes, Thomas Kent, Thomas Rickert, Victor Vitanza, and Lynn Worsham. In one way or another, all of these scholars wish to fundamentally alter the way the field thinks about teaching.

The problem is that the activity traditionally known as teaching (and, one hopes, the activity traditionally known as learning) will likely continue in some institutional form. That raises a fundamental question: how does composition, which has for so long defined itself as a teaching subject, reinvent the pedagogical portion of its mission without recourse to pedagogy as we have traditionally understood it? I doubt that many would deny that composition's research agenda should include more than teaching; the real question is how we talk about pedagogical work, in and out of the classroom, in the wake of this expanded agenda. If pedagogy is no longer our primary focus, how do we proceed with the work that takes up half of our professional lives? How do we teach after pedagogy? Answering that question is the project of this book.

My method of answering the question does not reject postpedagogy but rather accepts it as a starting point. Postpedagogical arguments are penetrating, even disturbing, and they demand something more nuanced than simple disagreement. I want to argue *with* these scholars, both to dispute and to deliberate. After all, my central question—What does it mean to teach after pedagogy?—could not be articulated without the argument they have occasioned. Yet I also refuse the suggestion that pedagogy is a self-defeating pursuit. Surely composition has the scholarly resources to talk about teaching as an intellectual enterprise. Thus my initial return to Phelps, who attempts to articulate a pedagogy rigorous in its attention to resources and responsiveness.

Yet turning to Phelps raises other issues. Why, for example, has her cultivation of *phronesis* (by way of Freire, Gadamer, and Dewey) not taken deep root? There may be several answers to this question. Among the most important, I would suggest, is that *phronesis* has often been superseded or undermined by epistemological concerns. Our field's interpretation of Freire, for example, has often assumed that new ways of knowing would result in new ways of doing. In fact, objections to that epistemological assumption—particularly the version expressed by James Berlin—have occasioned a great deal of postpedagogical discourse, particularly in the work of Hawk, Rickert, and Vitanza. The same could be said for hermeneutics, as Raúl Sánchez observes in *The Function of Theory in Composition Studies.* Hermeneutics, Sánchez argues, still believes that writing *represents* some other reality rather than being a reality in and of itself. Sánchez objects to this essentialism, which "reserves systemic and uncritical conceptual space for *something* nondiscursive" (92). This attitude—which, Sánchez argues, is also forwarded by Berlin—reduces writing to a "notation system of experience" and rhetoric to "the dress of thought" (47). Casuistically stretched to pedagogy, Sánchez's objections would caution us against seeing the pedagogical situation as a text to be interpreted for its meaning.[1] Ultimately, Gadamer's hermeneutics may do a great deal to justify composition as a human science rather than a hard science. But it also may inadvertently distance us from what actually happens (or ought to happen) in pedagogy: the invention of writing (rather than the interpretation of it). In addition to these difficulties, there is the basic conceptual difficulty contained in the idea of *phronesis* itself, the problem of imagining the sort of wisdom that is triggered by a situation that has not yet occurred.

Of Phelps's original triumvirate, then, we are left with Dewey and his idea of "experience," which, I argue, offers the most productive available means for doing the work of teaching after pedagogy.[2] Teaching begins neither in practice nor in theory, but in experience. New teachers, for example, have little to go on except experience, as Erika Lindemann observes: "They *remember how they were taught*; they read; they listen to others suggest what writing courses ought to do—but evaluating the information is difficult. Until they develop a conceptual framework to help them sort out what they read and hear, *they must teach by trial and error*" (3; emphasis added). As we accumulate experience, its power becomes more alluring. Paul Kameen articulates this desire in *Writing/Teaching*: "I'm sure many share the feeling that I've had, quite often, after I've finished teaching a course for the first time: that I wish I could go back and do it over, but with the knowledge I have right now. Not next term or next year, but to go back in time with the same people, the same books. Smarter, this time, though" (131). The ultimate teacher's dream: to teach a particular course with the experience of already having taught that particular course. Wouldn't it be wonderful if, like a pedagogical Bill Murray in *Groundhog Day*, we could anticipate every difficulty, every misunderstanding, and every stumble and then head them off with perfect, brilliant aplomb? (Sure, there is the risk of suicidal ennui, but just think of the teaching evaluations.)

As Kameen understands, such a world is neither attainable nor desirable since such a world makes growth impossible. We can only be smarter *next* time, which means that the smarts we have attained through our experience have to be revised and repurposed. Kameen insists, "It's important to recognize the degree to which what a course actually teaches is not necessarily confined to the time it takes to complete it. . . . Somewhere down the line my thinking about [a course] will make a difference" (131). Ann Berthoff insists that the "most useful slogan for the composition course" is "*Ex nihilo nihil fit*: out of nothing, nothing can be made" ("Learning"

76). The challenge, therefore, is to make something new out of the something we already have. Berthoff's motto makes pedagogy "post" in a literal sense—that is, pedagogy is the work that follows classroom activity rather than precedes it. What we should be asking ourselves, in other words, is the *Tuesday* Morning Question: what do we do on Tuesday morning with the experience of Monday morning? Pedagogy is not the first step; it is the second. It is a "sundown activity," similar to what Gustavo Gutiérrez describes in *Theology of Liberation:*

> Theology is reflection, a critical attitude. Theology *follows;* it is the second step. What Hegel used to say about philosophy can likewise be applied to theology: it rises only at sundown. The pastoral activity of the Church does not flow as a conclusion from theological premises. Theology does not produce pastoral activity; rather it reflects upon it. (9)

One need not believe in the Church, liberatory pedagogy, or even Hegelian dialectic to recognize the appropriateness of Gutiérrez's idea for the present discussion. With a couple of key substitutions, we can invent a vision for the Tuesday Morning Question: "*Pedagogy* follows; it is the second step. . . . It rises only at sundown. The *teaching* of *composition* does not flow as a conclusion from *pedagogical* premises. *Pedagogy* does not produce *teaching;* rather it reflects upon it." Pedagogy is not what we do before we enter the classroom or even while we're there. It is what we do after we leave. Both preposition and adjective, the *after* in *After Pedagogy* refers not only to our contemporary conversation—in which we are skittish about discussing pedagogy at all—but also to a kind of teaching that focuses on how we work with experience that has already occurred. Pedagogy is something we pursue; instead of it following us, we follow it. Our work—literally "post"—is to engage that which is occasioned by our students' work.

Dewey, whose ultimate keyword is *experience*, offers guidance as to how we might make a habit of the Tuesday Morning Question, how we might be smarter next time and how we might make something else out of something. For Dewey, experience is the moment, what we have taught them, as though our lessons can be carried in a case. Dewey's notion of experience suggests that what we learn enters into an ecology that immediately reshapes and grants significance to that experience. Thus Dewey's notion of experience offers a way to think about the Tuesday Morning Question. Postpedagogy would have us concentrate our attention on recognizing moments of emergence; Dewey would remind us that such moments are meaningful only insofar as they are incorporated into future possibility. Dewey thus provides the theoretical grounds for continually rethinking and renewing teaching after pedagogy. His philosophy actually begins in praxis—that is, it assumes that practice and theory cannot be divided in our actual experience of the world. They are concomitant and coequal. Because they are so often divided for purposes of analysis, however, the difficulty lies in articulating a praxis that captures the full complexity of their interaction.

For this purpose, I turn to casuistry in Chapter 4, "Unprincipled Pedagogy." Casuistry is a method of case-based reasoning designed for situations in which two values, goods, or rules conflict. Its usefulness for pedagogy is in its taxonomic method of interpreting situations. Casuistry sees experience as a repertoire of response, a repertoire shaped by particular sensitivity to the new situation. A pedagogical casuistry would therefore allow teachers to bring the given and the new into productive relationship. To be sure, casuistry is a counterintuitive choice for a method. For many, the term itself is arcane and obscure; for many others, casuistry is a synonym for manipulation and deceit. Though its roots can be traced to Aristotle, its reputation has been in decline since the seventeenth century. In between, casuistry became a common form of moral deliberation in the Catholic Church, most closely associated with the Jesuits (whose own name, like casuistry, became a byword for sophistry). In spite of this historical baggage, I turn to casuistry because it is essentially a method of practical reasoning whose self-correcting check is the complexity of experience itself. Applied to teaching, casuistry can balance the (sometimes) competing claims of *kairos* and pedagogy. Composition may no longer believe that we can or should produce pedagogy, but that does not mean we cannot have a rigorous pedagogical conversation, a conversation tied to the actual experience of teaching.

Most important, casuistry offers pedagogy a method of practical wisdom. Unfortunately, "method" and "practical wisdom" are more often opposed than they are linked. Depending on one's perspective, method either obviates or stifles practical wisdom; practical wisdom either supplements or compensates for method. Like so many either–or distinctions, this is a false choice. Method is not so generalizable that it cannot be fashioned for particular situations, and situations are not so particular that they cannot be reshaped through method. *After Pedagogy* assumes that practical wisdom itself is produced through the intervention of method. We discern how our old experience does or does not fit new experience, how new experience does or does not fit old assumptions. We experience, we reflect, we shape and reshape action through reflection on past experience. This basic method, which Dewey would call both empirical and practical, guarantees nothing, but uncertainty does not undermine wisdom. In the realm of praxis, wisdom without uncertainty is not wisdom at all. The once and future challenge to teaching is to articulate our wisdom with and within this uncertainty.

ACKNOWLEDGMENTS

THIS IS ESSENTIALLY A BOOK ABOUT LEARNING through example. That I should write such a book is not surprising, since I have been blessed with the finest exemplars. I hope this work lives up to them.

I first owe thanks to the dissertation committee who originally encouraged my odd project on casuistry. To Patricia Sullivan, who continues in her role as director, teacher, and mentor long after my graduation. To Richard Johnson Sheehan, who has also been a mentor and friend since I began graduate school in New Mexico. Thanks, too, to the other members of my committee: David Blakesley, Thomas Rickert, and Irwin Weiser.

Gratitude is also owed to Saint Louis University, particularly the Office of the Vice President for Academic Affairs for awarding me a leave, without which this project would not have been possible.

Thanks to my colleague and friend Nathaniel Rivers, whose insight (and presence) has been essential to the completion of this project. Thanks, too, to Saint Louis University colleagues Sara van den Berg and Jim Voiss. And to Emily Tuttle, an extraordinarily careful proofreader.

Thanks to Joe Harris, who offered guidance at key moments of this project's composition.

To the editors of *Pedagogy*, special thanks for permission to republish part of "Unprincipled Pedagogy" (11.2 [2011]: 257–83).

Finally, and most important, thanks to my wife, Melody, a reader of incisive perception and a listener of infinite patience. Her generosity defies *copia*. And to our daughter, Beatrice.

1

Inspired Adhoccery

> The only way out is through.
> —Richard E. Miller, *Writing at the End of the World*

NOTHING BEFORE AND NOTHING BEHIND

IN BOOK XII OF HIS *Institutes of Oratory,* Quintilian finally turns from system building to the deeper problem of developing the *vir bonus dicendi peritus,* the good man speaking well. As he shifts from what he wants an orator to do to who he wants the orator to be, Quintilian's confidence in his project begins to erode:

> Subsequently I was lured still further on my voyage by the temptations of the favoring breeze that filled my sails; but the rules which I was then concerned to give were still of a familiar kind and had been already treated by most writers of rhetorical textbooks: thus far I seemed to myself to be still in sight of shore and I had the company of many who had ventured to entrust themselves to the self-same winds. But presently when I entered on the task of setting forth a theory of eloquence which had been but newly discovered and rarely essayed, I found but few that had ventured so far from harbour. And finally now . . . I begin to feel how far I have been swept into the great deep. Now there is "Nothing before and nothing behind but the sky and the Ocean." (XII: 353, 355)

After hundreds of pages of cradle-to-grave curriculum design, Quintilian finds himself at sea. Who can rhetoric teach you to be? Answering this question is like losing sight of shore. Quintilian looks for assurance in the experience of Aeneas, who came to the banks of the Tiber only after many difficult voyages and false land-ings.[1] The only exemplar that Quintilian can perceive is Cicero, and "even he, though the ship in which he entered these seas is of such size and so well found, begins to lessen sail and to row a slower stroke" (XII: 4). Despite his trepidation, Quintilian senses that he cannot shelter in the harbor of his exhaustive plan of study. Yet his dismissal of the preceding Herculean labor as "comparatively trivial details" (XII: 353) seems a startling admission about the nature of education: it is easy to design a curriculum, even a life-sized cur-riculum, but it is much harder to know exactly what or whom that curriculum will produce.

Earlier in the treatise, Quintilian offers what may be *the* under-statement of the Western rhetorical tradition:

> Let no one however demand from me a rigid code of rules such as most authors of textbooks have laid down, or ask me to impose on students of rhetoric a system of laws as immu-table as fate. . . . *If the whole of rhetoric could be thus embodied in one compact code, it would be an easy task of little compass,* but most rules are liable to be altered by the nature of the case. (II: xiii, 1–2; emphasis added)

The same can be said for teaching, particularly for teaching that hopes to inculcate some form of practical wisdom that can be man-ifested only in situations that the curriculum has not yet imagined. Seen from this perspective, education seems by its very nature too artificial to be of much use. John Muckelbauer puts the question: "Quite simply, if pedagogy is confined to particular classrooms in particular disciplines and particular institutions, can it justifiably claim to teach people how to respond in other settings?" (100). This is the basic problem of any rhetorical pedagogy, and it forces a stark choice on the would-be educator. You can choose the com-prehensive option of Quintilian and design a curriculum that tries to account for every moment of a rhetorical education and covers every theory that might inform those moments. This we might call the god's-eye view, in which the educator tries to comprehend a vast and deep curriculum in the same way the sea god might comprehend the ocean—totally, completely, magisterially. Yet even an attempt as grand as Quintilian's falters at the crucial moment. The other option is less ambitious. It takes what we might call the (Stanley) Fish's-eye view. From this perspective, teaching "situations" is impossible because we are always already teaching situations. As a result, we are left with "only a few worn and familiar bromides: practice makes perfect, you learn to write by writing, you must build on what you already know" (Fish, "Anti-Foundationalism" 355). This homespun advice lets us off the hook of having "something to say and something to sell" or of having to construct a theory to inform a practice (355). It also means that we do not have to worry about producing a cradle-to-the-grave metanarrative of the orator's development.

Yet this advice, however DIY, is not as humble as it sounds. Fish's version of anti-foundationalism suggests that we can import what we learn from one situation into another situation. If practice does indeed perfect, it is because we believe that previous experience improves future performance. To say "we already know more than we think" (355) is to suggest that we learn from situations even if we cannot always articulate that learning. There is no way for Fish, or anyone else, to repeat that dictum unless he has been able to shape a series of situations into some kind of semi-inductive conclusion, now enshrined in the helpfully alliterative slogan "practice makes perfect." Perhaps Fish is right to claim that there are no consequences to accepting the tenets of anti-foundationalism (353), but that may be because this kind of anti-foundationalism is not all that anti-foundational. The choice between the two visions of education—that of the sea-god and that of the fish—does not finally appear to be decisive. After all, each of these responses says, "Don't worry; either way you'll know what to do once you're in the deep." The only difference is in the nature of the plan, which may include either someone's attempt to map every inch of the ocean floor or a few handy maxims that might get us out of tight spots. The real choice may never have been between foundationalism and anti-foundationalism, but rather between quixotic ambition and blithe reassurance. Ultimately, however, the question of whether Fish is a secret foundationalist is not that interesting. What is more interesting, and more important, is whether we have two and only two choices about how to understand our own experience.

Two thousand years after Quintilian found himself adrift, Cynthia Haynes feels just as seasick as our ancient Roman colleague, "perched" as she is "on the bow of a small converted seal-hunting boat as it chugged straight into the Arctic Sea" (667). She has embarked on a whale-watching expedition, and now, in the turbulent waters and gray air, she wonders "what this Texan was doing on *this* boat" (667). Though she is there to look for whales, Haynes instead looks for a reason for embarking on a voyage that appears to be "against all logic" while she is "unable to take [her] eyes off the disappearing coastline, its security beckoning" (667). Like Quintilian, Haynes discerns in the vast expanse an occasion both for fear and for reflection on the enterprise of pedagogy. Just as she wonders what she is doing on this boat, she wonders what she is doing in "*this* field of rhetoric and composition" (668). She, too, associates the shore with the familiar rules and the vast and threatening sea with the deeper questions of rhetorical education. Unlike Quintilian, however, Haynes's deepest fear is not the water but the land. Rhetoric and composition, she insists, has

> kept too close to the shoreline, dragging the anchor of *argumentative writing* (a.k.a. critical thinking) until it took hold among the bedrock curricula of grammar and style, aims and modes, claims, grounds, and warrants. And now our most sound composition pedagogy has run *aground* like some leviathan, a beached whale that inexplicably (and paradoxically) crawls onto the shore—onto the ground of all ground, figuratively speaking. And thus begins our exhaustive search for the explicable in the inexplicable—the why, the reason, the rationale. . . . We can pile reason upon reason, answer upon answer, and still never know the *why*. (668)

Rhetoric and composition, she argues, is beset not by too little logic but by too much of it. "Critical thinking" has run us aground through its continued insistence on asking for reasons. Yet there are experiences—whale watching in the Arctic Sea perhaps being one of them—that do not succumb to reasons. Some things are to be appreciated rather than understood. Haynes quotes Angelus Silesius by way of Heidegger: "The rose is without why; it blooms because it blooms" (678). This claim appears to indulge some form of circular reasoning, but to point that out is to beg the question of why anyone should ask for such a reason. This need of reason, Haynes suggests, will be composition's undoing. The security of the coastline—whether in grammar, style, aims, modes, claims, warrants—is a siren's song.[2] Just as Quintilian discovers in his *Institutes*, the "trivial details" are simply not enough to encompass rhetoric.[3] "Teaching argument," Haynes writes, "amounts to sheltering students from the deep (and too fluid) regions of language (and Being). Yet we know (don't we) that writing should be strange, that we should feel alienated, removed, and detached from our *standard* habits of reading and thinking" (671). Discovering these "unstandard" ways requires that we sail out, rejecting what Michael Mendelson calls the "lingering Ramistic dream" (239) that Walter Ong has so thoroughly described. We must instead "unhinge the link between reason and pedagogy, and dissemble the assembly line model of education" (Haynes 673). Alienated, removed, detached . . . nothing before and nothing behind.

Haynes lends her voice to the chorus calling for a "pedagogy otherwise" (or pedagogy offshore), a way to think about teaching after we have concluded that pedagogy is no longer possible. Composition has heard these claims for two decades. In 1991, Victor Vitanza raised the question of whether writing should even be taught, and he insisted on a "moratorium on attempting to turn theory into praxis/pedagogy" ("Three" 160). In that same year (and same volume of essays by Harkin and Schilb, *Contending with Words*), Lynn Worsham rejected the "pedagogical imperative . . . requiring every theory of writing to translate into some pedagogical practice or at least some specific advice for teachers" (96). In 1993, Thomas Kent stated that "writing—conceived broadly as processes or bodies of knowledge—cannot be taught" (*Paralogic* 161). Though Vitanza, Worsham, and Kent draw different lessons from their reading (differences explored in Chapter 2), they come to the same conclusion about the possibility of pedagogy.

These calls for an end to pedagogy continue. In *Beyond Postprocess*, published twenty years after *Contending*, Sidney Dobrin, J. A. Rice, and Michael Vastola "contend that any move beyond postprocess be understood as inherently postpedagogy—not opposed to composition studies' pedagogical imperative, but more interested in questions and theories of writing not trapped by disciplinary expectations of the pedagogical" (13–14). In spite of this seeming caveat, these authors are opposed to composition's pedagogical imperative insofar as they share Worsham's perception of the field's tendency to forward the pedagogical at the expense of everything else. In *Postcomposition*, Dobrin writes that our new "mantra" ought to be "stop talking about teaching" (190). Not all those who I will label "postpedagogues" would echo this advice. But all would share a wariness and a weariness with any desire to discern the one true method. The field has been marked by a series of attempts to identify this method: Writing is a matter of removing the constraints of the social, or it is a matter of imposing them. Teaching is a matter of getting out of our students' way, or it is a matter of getting in their way. And before these small shifts, there was the ur-shift, which made the fundamental claim that a writing process could be discerned, described, and taught to others. As this claim became more inflated, its eventual collapse would be even more complete. Thus does the field become "postprocess," skeptical of any sweeping pedagogical program, and the teaching subject becomes marked—at least in some quarters—by its refusal to talk about teaching.[4]

How, then, does a field defined by a pedagogical mission reimagine itself without that mission? Obviously, this is a rhetorical question in the conventional sense of the word. Of course teaching will continue. Even if our research gaze turns away from the classroom, members of this field will still spend half their professional lives there. We therefore need a better question about how we think and talk about the work of teaching in the wake of postpedagogy. How do we untrain our capacity for system and paradigm? How do we theorize our teaching without succumbing to the pedagogical imperative? How do we teach after pedagogy?

It is tempting, at this point, to spend a great deal of time discussing the choice of "after" rather than "post." There is the obvious reason that it would be ridiculous to talk about being "postpostpedagogical." More important, the prefix *post* never really escapes the gravity of the word to which it is attached. To be postprocess is to operate out of the terms of process (and the quickest way to get people to talk about teaching is to tell them to stop). When I speak of being "after pedagogy," I do not mean to suggest some break by which composition can finally loose itself from pedagogy hope. In fact, I refer to the opposite of that desire. We can never be entirely free of such hope, and why, in any case, would we want to cut ourselves off from the resources that hope has inspired throughout the discipline's half century? But we can think about pedagogy differently, not just as what happens before we approach the classroom, but also what happens when we leave it. In a sense, I mean *after* not as a preposition but as an adjective. If we are to teach after pedagogy, we need to develop an after-pedagogy, in which pedagogy becomes not a way to teach in the familiar sense but rather a way to make a resource of our classroom experiences.[5]

My aim is not to debunk postpedagogy. Instead, my approach emulates Bruno Latour, who suggests that the critic "is not the one who debunks, but the one who assembles[,] . . . not the one who lifts the rugs from under the feet of the naive believers, but the one who offers the participants arenas in which to gather" (246). I want to think through the postpedagogical arguments—to assemble them in a pedagogical parlor—in order to deliberate about how we can even talk about teaching now. *Pace* Dobrin and his colleagues, there is some warrant for this project within postpedagogy itself. Gary Olson argues that after process, our classroom practices remain largely what they were: "Nothing pedagogically has changed. What changes is your own understanding of what you are doing in the classroom" ("Why" 427). My project seeks to discern what that changed understanding means for the work of teaching.

THE UNCERTAIN ROAD

What is pedagogy after pedagogy? How do we teach when any hope for a system of teaching has been undermined? How does one walk when there is no road?

Readers may recognize that last formulation from Antonio Machado's "Wanderer":

> Wanderer, your footsteps are
> the road, and nothing more;
> wanderer, there is no road,
> you make the road by walking.
> By walking one makes the road,
> and upon glancing behind
> one sees the path
> that never will be trod again.
> Wanderer, there is no road—
> only wakes upon the sea. (83–85)

Even those unfamiliar with the poem will know the proverb it has spawned: *We make the road by walking.*[6] The interpretation that produces this saying reverses the notion that principles should produce practice or that systems are the best way to address situations. To make the road by walking is to suggest that *how* produces *what,* or that *what* cannot be understood apart from *how,* or that the two are manifested together at the same moment. The road is created through walking, democracy through action, education through teaching and learning. This praxis-oriented interpretation of Machado's point has certainly been reassuring to teachers, who are so often faced with disruptions to our best laid plans. Our designs need not be flawless, for we teach by teaching. Yet the poem seems to undermine this comforting interpretation. Machado suggests that the road is also unmade by walking. The path that trails behind the walker disappears. She may be able to perceive the path: "upon glancing behind / one sees the path," but it is a path "that never will be trod again," either by the walker addressed in the poem or, it seems, by any other. We might be reassured that we can see the road behind us, but Machado denies even this fleeting retrospection. He shifts his metaphor from the solidity of ground to the fluidity of water: "there is no road—only wakes upon the sea." Once again, the sea becomes a metaphor representing uncertainty. Machado's invocation of the waves offers a radical viewpoint on the nature of experience. Looking back, his walker is left to grasp at whitecaps, moments of emergence that quickly tumble back into the grey expanse. It is not just that we make the road as we go, but that the vision of the road we have left behind vanishes as quickly as it comes.

Though he was not talking about pedagogy, Machado's poem nevertheless warns the would-be teacher-reader against two kinds of pedagogy hope—one born of deduction and the other born of induction. We can neither apply principles (i.e., plan the road and then execute the plan), nor, it seems, form future plans (i.e., gather our experiences, remove them from the situation in which those experiences originally unfolded, and then apply them to some later situation—which ends up being another form of deduction). The former has usually been the greater source of trouble for composition. Witness the way in which process's early emphasis on experimentation and unfinishedness eventually hardened into a "pre hoc" algorithm. But the poem also suggests that post hoc assembly is no more reliable. Our experience of walking one road—which vanishes behind us—cannot be generalized to some other road. Nor can our road be left behind for someone else to walk. Postpedagogical arguments also resist pedagogy from this direction. Invention is too particular, too situated, too surprising; the attempt to learn from walking a road is like trying to capture the waves of the sea.

If we pursue pedagogy on Machado's unmade road, we are left with the conclusion that teaching can only ever happen within *uncertainty*, a word I use in the particular and radical sense offered by Michel Callon, Pierre Lascoumes, and Yannick Barthe in their *Acting in an Uncertain World: An Essay on Technical Democracy*. The authors draw a sharp and crucial distinction between *uncertainty* and *risk*. Risk, they write, "designates a well-identified danger associated with a perfectly describable event or series of events. We do not know if this event or series of events will in fact take place, but we know that it *may* take place" (19). In the imperishable formulation of Donald Rumsfeld, risk refers to "known unknowns" and therefore allows for some degree of rational decision. We can make a list of possible outcomes, describe the world—both the human and nonhuman entities—that will follow should any of those outcomes come to pass, and discern whether it will be feasible to live and operate in that possible world (19). With this information in hand, the decision maker can weigh the pros and cons and make a rational choice between the various options.

Uncertainty is far more unsettling than risk. In uncertainty, we cannot perceive or imagine the possible worlds that may result from our decisions: "We know that we do not know, but that is almost all that we know: there is no better definition of uncertainty" (Callon, Lascoumes, and Barthe 21). Donald Rumsfeld stumbles on a second true statement: "There are also unknown unknowns—the ones we don't know we don't know." These unknown unknowns resist rational decision. The kind of political–scientific hybrid problems that Callon and his coauthors examine do not lend themselves readily to risk analysis. Should we bury nuclear waste in a place where we can no longer reach it? Can people live near electromagnetic wiring without getting cancer? How do we know that medications that seem miraculous today won't turn out to cause defects and deformities twenty years from now? These questions do not admit simple risk assessment. Burying nuclear waste deep in the earth, beyond the reach of the mythical seventh generation, may not prove to be the best solution once that seventh generation arrives.

Compositionists have, perhaps haltingly, tried to confront this uncertainty in our own work. We know that certainty is not only unattainable but also undesirable, yet we also know that this uncertainty does not absolve us of the responsibility to act. Indeed, the paradox of uncertainty is that "we must take decisions—no one can avoid doing so—just when we are plunged into greatest uncertainty" (Callon, Lascoumes, and Barthe 1). Not knowing what the seventh generation—or the present generation—will want or need does not mean that we can indulge too long in hesitation. In the uncertain world, the model of the clear-cut decision disappears along with the oft-repeated myth of Alexander drawing his two-edged sword to cut the Gordian knot that no expert managed to untie. Sheathe your swords! This is the slogan that could sum up the now-famous principle of precaution. No more clear-cut, bloody decisions. Manly warrior assurance is not replaced by inaction, but by *measured action*, the only possible action in situations of high uncertainty. (11)

For some, it may be disappointing, even deflating, to consider that "measured action" is the most radical vision we can muster. (But then again, it is Aristotle, not Alexander, who is usually our hero.) We're not after conversion, nor enlightenment, nor give-me-a-first-year-student-when-he's-18-and-he's-mine-for-life, but measured action—cautious, fitful, hesitant. This milquetoast motto does have its promise, too. In *Counter-Statement*, Kenneth Burke writes, "A society is sound only if it can prosper on its vices, since virtues are by very definition rare and exceptional" (114). The vices he would endorse are the vices of democracy, which he defines as "organized distrust, 'protest made easy,' a babble of discordant voices, now endangered by the apostles of hope who would attack it for its 'inefficiency,' whereas inefficiency is the one thing it has in its favor" (114). In an uncertain world, perhaps these must be the prospering vices of measured action: organized distrust, protest, babble, discord, inefficiency. We might also call them the prospering vices of teaching after pedagogy, for they are likely to disrupt any attempt to recapture the lingering Ramistic dream.

In *The Function of Theory in Composition Studies*, Raúl Sánchez suggests that the field has tended to assume that theory is there to guide our work. As a result of this assumption, theory in composition studies has focused not on writing itself, but on how well writing or a given writing theory represents some other reality. "We firmly believe, despite our postmodern claims, in the presence of *something else* beyond the veil of language, and we have described it as being fundamentally apart from our language use, and we believe it to be theory's task to define and explain this noumenal realm" (10). The usual argument about composition theory has proceeded exactly along these lines: expressivism is said to represent our inner selves; cognitivism, the working of the mind; social constructionism, the influence of the community. Given this supposed division between reality and language, we can go on arguing theory without ever really encountering the full complexity of experience from which and within which writing happens. Translated into our pedagogical inquiry, Sánchez's idea reminds us that theory has often represented the desire for a certain kind of teaching efficiency. The conversation after pedagogy, however, must be judged by its *in*efficiency. There are virtues in this vice, as Paul Kameen suggests in *Writing/Teaching*. For Kameen, the *Protagoras* represents the sort of pedagogical conversation he is interested in having:

> a conversation in which the everyday desires and needs of teachers and students get addressed, haggled over, as fully and richly, in as polemical and particular terms as they are here in the argument between Socrates and Protagoras. And if in the process we can be, by turns, as eloquent, as comical, as fastidious, as earnest, as persnickety, as wise, as noble, as quixotic as these figures are in the hands of Plato, we will have gone a long way toward finding the sort of "discourse" that any contemporary field requires if it is to serve appropriately those who come to it, with the enthusiasm of Hippocrates, to "study professionally." (178)

Here we see the vices of organized pedagogical distrust: haggling, polemical argument. But we also see the virtues of such a conversation: eloquence, comedy, fastidiousness, earnestness, wisdom, nobility, and, of course, the quixotic hope that such a conversation matters in the first place. It is the kind of agon Debra Hawhee describes in *Bodily Arts*, the kind in which we are brought together by struggle. *Agon*, Hawhee reminds us, means both struggle/contest *and* gathering/assembly (15). This kind of conversation is particularly important in a postpedagogical field—a field once defined by pedagogy, a field that no longer wants to be limited to pedagogy, and a field in which pedagogy will nonetheless continue to play a large role. We know that we will teach, yet the conversation about teaching has sometimes limited and even distorted our vision of what we teach. We know that writing emerges in the doing and the *how*, yet the *how* question has often elicited methods and procedures that have calcified into various *whats*. We know that intellectual work extends beyond teaching, yet to dismiss teaching as somehow nonintellectual is to rely on a value system that has dismissed composition itself. The question then becomes what we're talking about when we're talking about pedagogy. If teaching is a road made by walking, how do we walk it without slipping into the rut of theory, which may remove us from the complexity of teaching, or the rut of practice, which may insert us into that complexity without recourse to reflection?

LIVING IN THE HOUSE OF LORE

The arena I imagine for this agon is described in Stephen North's *The Making of Knowledge in Composition*. North's taxonomy of compositionists includes honorific titles such as historians, critics, clinicians, scholars, philosophers, and, first (but not necessarily foremost), practitioners. This last group is made up of those for whom teaching is the primary work. "Practitioners are regarded essentially as technicians: Scholars and especially Researchers *make* knowledge; Practitioners apply it" (21). He acknowledges that this distinction does not serve the practitioner's academic reputation. The field, North claims, has become "largely unaccustomed to entertaining the notion of practice as a mode of inquiry at all" (21). Though he means to rehabilitate practical inquiry, North does not help the cause when he calls such knowledge *lore*, "what witches know, or herbal healers, or wizards in fantasy fiction" (23). North then offers a more professional definition of *lore*: "the accumulated body of traditions, practices, and beliefs in terms of which Practitioners understand how writing is done, learned, and taught" (22). He even outlines a sort of practice for lore: one identifies a problem, looks for causes, sees whether a given intervention works, and then tells people about it. This mirrors, in an informal way, the basic practices of intellectual inquiry.

In the end, though, North cannot help condescending, though gently, to lore. Consider his architectural metaphor:

> The House of Lore, as it were: a rambling, to my mind de-
> lightful old manse, wing branching off from wing, addition
> tacked to addition, in all sorts of materials—brick, wood,
> canvas, sheet metal, cardboard—with turrets and gables,
> minarets and spires, spiral staircases, rope ladders, pitons,
> dungeons, secret passageways—all seemingly random, yet all
> connected. Each generation of Practitioners inherits this pile
> from the one before, is ushered around some of what there is,
> and then, in its turn, adds on its own touches. Naturally, the
> structure is huge, sprawling. There are, after all, no provisions
> for tearing any of it down. (27)

As charming as this image is, it casts lore as essentially unmanage-
able. As long as the focus is practical, there appear to be no standards for tearing down any structure that lore has thrown up (24–
25). As the product of an oral tradition, lore simply accrues. In fact,
North argues that practitioner inquiry cannot really be rendered
in writing: "Reciprocity, of course—the interaction which, like a
gyroscope, serves to balance Practitioners in terms of structure and
logic—is essentially impossible; this is the stylized monologue with
a vengeance" (52–53). This suggests that North thinks it impossible to make a scholarly inquiry of such a conversation: "Practitioner knowledge very often gets presented with some of the trappings
of Scholars' or Researchers' inquiry, with confusion on both sides
over just what is being offered" (53). Lore can disguise itself with
the vestments of other methods, but such adornment serves only to
confuse. Delightful though it may be, lore is not scholarship.

These claims make a familiar distinction between thought and
everyday experience, as though to engage in the former requires
a separation from the latter. Unfortunately, this vision persists, as
Hephzibah Roskelly and Kate Ronald observe in *Reason to Believe.*
So great is the gulf, they argue, that composition has

> two different disciplinary communities, two ways of seeing
> the "action" required of teachers of writing. Practitioners, left
> only with "lore," focus on examining classroom experience,
> studying students' experience, and generalizing from there

about overall methods; theorists, enthralled mostly in texts
and models, focus on examining relationships out of context,
sometimes without looking at all to their own or their students'
experience. (16; emphasis added)

These authors acknowledge that many who work in composition
defy this division. There is no doubt that rigorous pedagogical
scholarship can still be found in composition, including the scholars whose work I address in this project: Haynes, Vitanza, Kent,
Kameen, Diane Davis, Thomas Rickert, Byron Hawk, among others. At the same time, pedagogy and the classroom experience hold
an increasingly precarious position in composition. David Bartholomae, for example, worries that student writing is disappearing
from our scholarship (Bartholomae and Schilb 279). And as we
have seen, some would drop pedagogy as a disciplinary concern.
Dobrin, Rice, and Vastola dismiss any attempt to reconcile postprocess with composition's pedagogical concern as a "disciplinary
conservative project" that "terminates . . . in the lap of composition studies" (14–15) or that remains "nested in the safety of composition's pedagogical imperative, risking little of that disciplinary
comfort" (15). Unlike North's discussion of the old manse, here the
condescension is intentional and pointed.

Surely this is not the only way to think about pedagogy, as Sánchez suggests: "scholarly attention to classroom practice is entirely
appropriate and unquestionably necessary. . . . But just as writing
has been crucially reconceived to account for theoretical, empirical,
and pedagogical developments, so should pedagogy be reimagined"
("First" 191). Sánchez goes on to argue that pedagogy should be
seen as synonymous with culture. Citing Gramsci as his influence,
Sánchez holds that pedagogy goes beyond formal schooling and includes "the production and transmission of values at various levels
and locations of a given society" (192). The classroom, therefore,
becomes only one of many pedagogical sites. While it is the site
with which my argument is primarily concerned, I take Sánchez's
point that formal teaching can and should be reimagined. But if
we are to raze the division between pedagogy and culture, then

composition must turn lore into an intellectual project. North suggests such a theoretical possibility when he observes that one of the purposes of lore is "to frame, if you will—situations. . . . One of the purposes for any such body of knowledge is to make the otherwise overwhelming complexity of experience more manageable" (33). No doubt this is true, but the problem with the "delightful old manse" is that it continually outgrows whatever frames try to hold it. That is the nature of lore. How, then, can lore frame our experience without our demanding that lore itself become something that it is not?

This is the question Richard Fulkerson asks in his contribution to *The Changing of Knowledge in Composition*, a 25th anniversary reconsideration of North's landmark book. Fulkerson points to what he calls the "epistemic cocoon" that surrounds lore. In North's metaphor, no wing of the House of Lore can ever be dismantled; there are no provisions for challenging lore claims. This is a problem, reasons Fulkerson, if lore wishes to be considered epistemology. "What North needed but could not find or develop was some fair way of distinguishing credible lore from incredible" (52). Fulkerson claims that no one else has, either. If we can assess the content claims of lore, however, then lore seems to lose any epistemological claim to being a unique form of knowledge and becomes nothing more than a bad form of ethnography. The choice is uninviting. It is as if the notion of "empiricism" commits us to unraveling the texture of our own classroom experience. Of course, Fulkerson is not endorsing such an outcome, though he is worried that "the field's future is endangered by its totalizing embrace of lore done well [i.e., ethnography]" (61). Narratives might be enjoyable, but they are not all to be considered knowledge. "I love reading teacher narratives," writes Fulkerson, "even though I try to avoid drawing propositional conclusions" (61). Though it would seem strange not to draw any propositional conclusions from books such as *Lives on the Boundary, Bootstraps,* or *Voices of the Self,* Fulkerson's point is a good one: if there are no grounds for challenging a lore claim—if lore is essentially unprovable—how can it be said to be knowledge at all?

THE PRACTICE OF EXPERIENCE

Fulkerson's basic question is this: Can we speak of method and lore in the same context without putting scare quotes around either word? Or, as I wish to put the question, can we make a method of lore? These questions reflect postpedagogical skepticism of rhetoric as a teachable art. At the same time, we know that we often succeed in teaching. Particular assignments or lessons or activities do work, even if saying "the kids seemed to love it" is not a persuasive claim. Unfortunately, the ways we narrate these successes cannot be considered knowledge unless they are translated into some form that guarantees their repeatability; yet that translation is the very thing that risks undermining their sensitivity to particularity and situation. We are left, then, with a collection of stories, unable to express or to analyze them in a way that makes them a resource. In effect, we are cut off from our own experience. The only thing we can do is what Ann Berthoff calls "recipe-swapping":

> You know how it is; it has certainly happened to me. You hear something described that sounds good; it's obviously foolproof; you try it, and it doesn't work. So you feel terrible because this great exercise is a proved success—and you flubbed it. By reminding us that reading and writing happen in contexts—social, political, psychological—that can set up static ruinous to the reception of the very best assignments, theory can save us wasting time blaming ourselves or our students. (*Making* 34)

Every reader of this book can probably recall an experience like the one Berthoff describes. Without the abstraction of theory, Berthoff argues, lessons from one context cannot simply be grafted on to another. If lore is to be useful, then, we do have to abstract from it. Yet we also must account for its specificity. Otherwise, we cannot fit our abstractions into their new contexts. Unless we can see the specifics of the original situation, it is impossible even to abstract in the first place. Paradoxically, the only way to abstract is to pay attention to particularity.

What we need, then, is a term that captures the paradox of abstraction and particularity. For this purpose, I nominate *experience*. Specifically, I rely on John Dewey's notion of experience, "a concept that Dewey invokes in *every other area of his philosophy*" (Hildebrand 9). For Dewey, experience can be understood as both primary and ultimate, "primary as it is given in an uncontrolled form, ultimate as it is given in a more regulated and signified form—a form made possible by the methods and the results of reflective experience" (*Experience and Nature* 15). Dewey's idea of experience includes the everyday world and the methodical reflection that infuses that everyday world with meaning. Thus, Dewey does not see a division between mind and world, individual and environment, thought and action. There is no such thing as purely "raw" experience since no one can experience the world without also being conditioned by language, culture, and habit. But the fact that experience comes precooked does not mean that we are prevented from further experimentation. My argument—one on which I expand in Chapter 3—is that Dewey's idea of experience offers composition a way to make a method of lore, to make method an intellectual project, and to talk and write about teaching after pedagogy.

Dewey's lifelong project was to break down philosophic or theoretical dualisms that could no longer plausibly represent human experience. His *Quest for Certainty*, for example, offers a sustained critique of the split between theory and practice, which, he argues, developed out of basic material and physical insecurity:

> As long as man was unable by means of the arts of practice to direct the course of events, it was natural for him to seek an emotional substitute; in the absence of actual certainty in the midst of a precarious and hazardous world, men cultivated all sorts of things that would give them the *feeling* of certainty. (*Later* 26)

The location of certainty outside of the precarious and hazardous world characterizes both ancient and modern philosophy. We still assume, he writes, "that certainty, security, can be found only in the fixed and unchanging[,] . . . that knowledge is the only road to that which is intrinsically stable and certain[,] . . . that practical activity is an inferior sort of thing" (41). Though this tendency was once understandable, it can no longer be the basis for a philosophy in a world of constant change.

Rejecting the distinction between theory and practice as false, Dewey defines thought as "a mode of directed overt action" rather than "a property of something termed intellect or reason apart from nature" (*Later* 133). This unification of thought and action finds its way everywhere in his work, particularly in his writing on education, where Dewey insists schooling has to be united with practical affairs. This argument had often led to misconceptions about his ideals; Dewey is hardly the "child-centered," content-free hippie his detractors sometimes make him out to be. "Nothing is more absurd," he writes, "than to suppose that there is no middle term between leaving a child to his own unguided fancies and likes or controlling his activities by a formal succession of dictated directions" (*School* 130). Dewey nominated many candidates for that middle term: *communication, transaction, reflection*. All three suggest the complex interplay between the factors through which and in which education happens: the young person, the older person, and the "aims, meanings, and values" they do or do not share:

> It is easier to see the conditions in their separateness, to insist upon one at the expense of the other, to make antagonists of them, than to discover a reality to which each belongs. . . . When this happens a really serious practical problem—that of interaction—is transformed into an unreal, and hence insoluble, theoretic problem. Instead of seeing the educative steadily as a whole, we see conflicting terms. We get the case of the child *vs* the curriculum; of the individual *vs* social culture. Below all other divisions in pedagogic opinion lies this opposition. (*School* 182–83)

This is the very division that leads to the failures of recipe-swapping, which simply divorces practice from theory. To put it in Charles Taylor's terms, recipe-swapping divorces ad hoc practice from the inspiration that might animate it. Dewey insists that inspiration has to be manifested within "adhockery" even to qualify as inspiration at all. As ever, Dewey rejects the idea that psychology can "form a separate and isolated mental world in and of itself, self-sufficient and self-enclosed" (*Experience and Nature* 15). Rather, experience travels between mind and world, individual and environment, and encompasses both.

Even more important for the present project, Dewey's idea offers the possibility of *renewal* and *continuity*. Both of these concepts suggest that the venture of making the road by walking can become a part of other walking and other roads. The road may disappear behind us, but our experience of it does not. What we do with that experience determines the later use we might make of it. For Dewey, the central question of education is this: "How shall the young become acquainted with the past in such a way that the acquaintance is a potent agent in appreciation of the living present?" (*Experience and Education* 23). He defines *education* as the "reconstruction or reorganization of experience which adds to the meaning of experience, and *which increases ability to direct the course of subsequent experience*" (*Democracy* 76; emphasis added). Our present experience is inspired not only by the primary event but also by the ultimate meaning lent by previous experience. We can investigate experience, or we can ignore it; either way, it shapes the meaning of everyday life.

My ultimate question—what I see as *the* question for a postpedagogical discipline like composition—is this: *how shall we cultivate experience in order to foster growth* (particularly our own growth, but perhaps our students' as well)*?* Of course, there is no single answer to this question, a surmise that at first glance seems to leave us right where we started: a pile of situations with no way to learn from them. This has often seemed to be the plight of a teaching discipline shaped by lore, as Berthoff describes in "Rhetoric as Hermeneutic":

> We go from sentence combining to freewriting and back again to the formal outline; from vague notions of "pre-writing" to vaguer notions of heuristics; from rigid rubrics to the idea of no writing at all. Some might celebrate this *uncertainty*

as evidence of pluralism and a lack of dogmatism in the field, *but it could also be characterized as a distracted, purposeless, and despairing adhocism.* An idea which one year is everywhere hailed and celebrated vanishes the next year without a trace. (279; emphasis added)

I do not read Berthoff as arguing for a simpler time when men were men, women were women, and process was process. Clearly, it is not the adhocism itself that drives her to despair so much as the distracted and purposeless way in which we pursue that adhocism. Given our current philosophical and theoretical impasse—in which the very idea of pedagogy or paradigm hope has lost its power—it is easy to imagine a regress to despairing adhocism. To one entering the discipline today, it may well seem that composition has spent its first fifty years simply charting its uncertainties. (You could do worse for an intellectual achievement.) But once again, we are left with seemingly untenable choices: either we suffer an intolerable uncertainty about what we do, or we cling to whatever keeps us afloat for the given moment.

We can also decide that these are not our only choices. Finally, then, we come to my particular recipe, or rather my way of deliberating between recipes. This one is borrowed, but it will be thoroughly theorized. I am speaking of *casuistry,* the West's oldest method of case-based moral reasoning. The term itself comes from the Latin *casus,* or case, which indicates the main feature of casuistry's way of proceeding. It is particularly useful in situations where two duties, obligations, or values conflict. When confronting an ethical conundrum, casuists begin with the particular case rather than with the rulebook. They make a decision that fits that case so well that it cannot be easily changed into a rule for deciding future cases. As its etymology suggests, casuistry has long been a part of legal reasoning and, more recently, of medical reasoning. Unfortunately, the idea of casuistry is beset by a troubling combination of obscurity and infamy. Most people are unfamiliar with the term, and those who are likely equate it with the worst kinds of manipulation and rationalization. Though casuistry was once a common method of moral reasoning, it has fallen into disuse since the seventeenth century, when Pascal's *Provincial Letters* almost single-handedly destroyed its reputation. When people do recognize the term, they are likely to associate it with popery, wizardry, sophistry, and harlotry (Jonsen and Toulmin 11). In *Casuistry and Modern Ethics,* Richard B. Miller writes, "Casuistry has no place in religion or ethics, many people say, because it is a form of chicanery" (4). In spite of these problems, casuistry has occasionally experienced brief rehabilitations in the contemporary period. Following Albert Jonsen and Stephen Toulmin's 1989 *The Abuse of Casuistry,* a vigorous reexamination ensued in the field of medical ethics, where clinicians struggle every day to match moral theories to particular difficulties. And of course case-based reasoning has always played a role in law. The best contemporary articulation of the casuistic style in legal thought was offered in Cass Sunstein's 1998 *Legal Reasoning and Political Conflict.* Both Sunstein and Jonsen and Toulmin suggest that casuistry's most important feature is its backgrounding of principle and its foregrounding of particularity. By concentrating on the case, they argue, deliberators can worry less about clashing ideologies and more about practical problem solving.

The problem that casuistry tries to address is also the problem that pedagogy has tried to address: "If practical argument is, by definition, anchored in the concrete details of specific cases, how do we generalize about effective practice, or more to the present point, how do our students learn to make sound judgments under conditions that are infinitely variable?" (Mendelson 234). Yet while I think this an important question, it is not quite the one I wish to answer, since it suggests that pedagogy is a problem that needs solving. Rather, I want to devise a method (as Berthoff understands the term) of intellectualizing experience (as Dewey understands it) in a way that enriches future experience. My argument is that casuistry's case-based methodology, its reliance on maxim and analogy, and its willingness to rearticulate what seems settled and sure all offer a methodology that can sustain the postpedagogical project.

Rather than a despairing adhocism, I am searching for a kind of *inspired adhoccery.* I borrow this formulation from Charles Taylor, who coined it in a 1989 article on the Salman Rushdie controversy.

Taylor's piece concerned the decision by authorities in India to censor *The Satanic Verses*. Was it right, Taylor asks, that Indian officials had banned the book in order to prevent deadly rioting? Though Taylor counts himself a defender of free speech, he cannot quite bring himself to side with Rushdie, who excoriated the decision. Rushdie's response, writes Taylor, ignored the real risk of violence if the book was released at that particular moment: "There are things which are so inflammatory that they are a danger to public order, to life and limb" (118). Taylor can thus admit the possibility that there might be an occasion for doing something as illiberal as suppressing a book, even temporarily. It is easy to say, "Do justice and let the skies fall." It is harder when you fear that the skies might actually fall. How, then, do we draw the line—or the many lines— that might need to be drawn for many different situations? Taylor writes, "There isn't a universal definition of freedom of expression, because there isn't a single world culture. We are going to have to live with this pluralism for some time. That means accepting solutions for one country which don't apply in others. . . . We are going to need some inspired adhoccery in years to come" (121). Though Taylor does not spend much time teasing out the meanings of his phrase, his use of it suggests the ability to make a temporary decision when circumstances present incommensurable choices.

Stanley Fish then elaborated on this idea in *The Trouble with Principle*:

> What [inspired adhoccery] means is that the solutions to particular problems will be found by regarding each situation-of-crisis as an opportunity for improvisation and not as an occasion for the application of rules and principles (although the invoking and the recharacterizing of rules and principles will often be components of the improvisation). Any solution devised in this manner is likely to be temporary—that is what ad hoc means—and when a new set of problems has outstripped its efficacy, it will be time to improvise again. (63–64)

Given Fish's anti-foundationalism, this gloss on Taylor's term emphasizes the adhocness over the inspiration. Fish speaks of "particular" problems, of "improvisation" rather than "application," of the temporary over the permanent.

Yet rules also have a role to play as inspiration for ad hoc decisions. Our improvisations are shaped by our principles—whether those principles are articulated in propositional content or in ethical commitment. In *Educating the Reflective Practitioner,* Donald Schön describes the kind of inspiration compositionists might cultivate. In addition to having professional knowledge, practitioners in any field also share an "'appreciative system'—the system of values, preferences, and norms in terms of which they can make sense of practice situations, formulate goals and directions for action, and determine what constitutes acceptable professional conduct" (33). Practitioner knowledge is always "bounded by commitments to appreciative system and overarching theory" (*Reflective* 166). It makes decisions on the fly but does so within a larger vision of what should constitute good practice. Without such inspiration, there would be little reason to improvise at all, little reason to find temporary solutions when our rules and principles prove inadequate for a given situation. As Fish suggests, however, those same rules and principles are not utterly recalcitrant; they, too, can be recharacterized and rethought in light of new situations.

"Theory hope" does not lurk in this description. Fish's idea of inspired adhoccery thus avoids the problems of deduction and induction. We cannot simply apply rules to situations, but neither can we abstract rules from situations (for later deductive application). The "adhocness" is too situated and complex—"always on the wing"— to allow either possibility. To put the matter in Burkean rather than Fishian terms: while the interpretive trout can revise its distinction between bait and food, "a different kind of bait may outwit him, if it lacks the appearance by which he happens to distinguish 'jaw-ripping food'" (*Permanence* 5). To form an either-or, deductive premise from a jaw-ripping experience would only delay being caught. To then put the matter in Deweyan terms, new experience constantly reshapes our principles. To be "inspired," in this sense, is to be in dialogue with what we believed prior to new experience, or to check that new experience against what we believed. Dewey's basic test it this: "Does [a philosophy, a theory] end in conclusions which, when they are referred back to ordinary life-experiences and their predicaments, render them more significant, more luminous to us, and make our dealings with them more fruitful?" (*Experience and Nature* 7). In this sense, *inspiration* is another word for Berthoff's "meaning," which is always discerned through the ad hoc activity of practical experience.

Inspired adhoccery, translated as casuistry, offers a way past the dualisms that trouble composition's pedagogical conversation. We need not settle for adhoccery or adhocism as the best we can do, nor need we be content with pedagogy as a mere motley of lessons that somehow "worked" at some point in the past. And yet adhoccery itself is not enough, for it will always be inspired by some imaginative impulse, an impulse that Berthoff calls our "chief speculative instrument" (*Making* 28). We can bring some method to that particular kind of madness, but method need not encourage a false hope in any paradigm. Inspired adhoccery offers a stance that could sustain a pedagogical conversation, for it demands both a response to a situation and a response to the theory we bring to a situation. Ultimately, the project of this book is to invent this sort of pedagogical imagination.

2

Is Teaching Still Impossible?

> It is difficult for any of us to relinquish the idea that we, as members of the education mechanism, are not forwarding the process of education. The simple proclamation "I teach" is lifted from our repertoire, according to these theories, as the act of teaching is no longer possible.
> —Sidney I. Dobrin, "Paralogic Hermeneutic Theories, Power, and the Possibility for Liberating Pedagogies"

THE 19TH ENDNOTE

COMPOSITION HAS FACED MANY PROVOCATIVE challenges to its conventional pedagogical wisdom (including the epigraph of this chapter). Among the most powerful is Cynthia Haynes's 2003 "Writing Offshore: The Disappearing Coastline of Composition Theory." Drawing upon a nearly disorienting array of resources—including oceanography, Heideggerian philosophy, international politics, postmodern architecture, Christian mysticism, Irish and German poetry, critical theory, and, of course, rhetoric and composition—Haynes implores composition to reconsider the role of argumentation in our pedagogy. Her point is straightforward: though argument (along with variants such as "critical thinking," "reasoning," and "grounds") has long enjoyed unquestioned status as composition's fundamental mode of thinking, argument should now be up for argument. She laments that argumentation "has become the *capstone* of composition" (669). It is a capstone Haynes would like to roll away.

Her reason? A lack of reason: "that post-9/11 face of disbelief, disenchantment, and disaffection for writing arguments when *so much defies reason*" (Haynes 669). What rational explanation could account for the everyday horrors of the contemporary world? "Airplanes hit towers, and structures implode with people in them . . . while boat people sabotage their own boats, desperate for rescue" (669). Given the groundlessness of this suffering, what argument—however well grounded, however well reasoned—could possibly respond? Certainly, there is a logic to many acts we might label "unreasonable." The 9/11 hijackers did not pick the World Trade Center and the Pentagon out of a hat, and boat people are thinking quite reasonably when they sabotage their own boats to force a rescue. If these acts are the wages of reason, Haynes argues, perhaps it is time to free ourselves and our students from that economy. Unfortunately, rhetoric and composition has yet to divest itself. Haynes writes that "we [composition] kept too close to the shoreline, dragging the anchor of *argumentative writing*" and that "our most sound composition pedagogy has run *aground* like some leviathan" (668). She wants composition to "write offshore," to cast itself beyond the safety of reason so that we may encounter new ways of writing and thinking for which reason cannot account.

If we were to follow Gerald Graff's suggestion that complex arguments be occasionally sound-bited for simplicity and clarity, Haynes's could be captured in one word: *stop.* Stop chasing what Michael Mendelson has called the "lingering Ramistic dream" (239). That dream, Haynes writes, holds that "reason is perfected in pedagogy, for pedagogy, by pedagogues" (673). Just as the Sabbath was made for man, and not man for the Sabbath, so too reason was made for people, and not people for reason. Since at least Ramus, however, pedagogy has forgotten this. Haynes here turns to Walter Ong, who writes this in his work on Ramus:

> In the university world before and during Ramus' time, dialectic itself, which in its etymological origin was concerned with real dialogue[,] . . . was habitually thought of as implementing not dialogue, but *the huge pedagogical apparatus.* As the "instrument" of intellectual activity, it became assimilated to the particular intellectual activity being served. Instead of representing an approach to truth through the real dialectic of Socratic midwifery, or through a series of probabilities as in

Aristotle's conception, dialectic or "logic" became the subject *a teacher taught to other coming teachers in order to teach them how to teach, in their turn, still other apprentice teachers, and so on ad infinitum.* (154; emphasis added)

Haynes's argument is that rhetoric and composition must detach itself from this apparatus. Rather than asking students to resist ideology or conventional wisdom, Haynes "would place in students' hands the *power to resist teaching itself*" so that they may "unhinge the link between reason and pedagogy, and dissemble the assembly line model of education in whose grip we have been since Ramus so cleanly paired discourse and logic" (673; emphasis added). Perhaps *Resist Teaching!* offers a more accurate sound bite than *stop*, but the idea is the same either way: step off the assembly line.

The problem, however, is how to detach from one apparatus without offering another in its place. How do we speak of what comes next? After the pedagogical moratoria of Vitanza and Worsham, it seems impossible to speak unself-consciously of a new "way" to teach. It also seems impossible to detach from one apparatus without proposing something in its place. Haynes senses this problem, and she carefully couches the one "practical" suggestion (i.e., Monday Morning Answer) that she offers:

Heeding Vitanza's moratorium on turning theory into praxis, yet mindful of the urgency of deregulating the argumentation industry that has our field so tightly in its grip, I offer the following assignment in the spirit of my title—writing offshore. Give your students (or yourselves) this *depth probe* assignment: Write something offshore (that is, put a message in a bottle) in response to this statement: *WE ARE ALL BOAT PEOPLE.* Now take your paper and make a paper boat. Leave it in a prominent place such as a doorstep, a computer terminal, the university administration building, or wear it on your clothes, whatever. Then imagine its trajectory, where it will go, who will see it, what they will think (what you would *like* them to think). And then, put that in writing; trace the trajectories, and give it ballast—so that the main question you should ask yourself as you write is this: WILL IT FLOAT? (718)

This project does indeed invite students to resist teaching, for what teaching could prepare them for this assignment? Yes, the assignment does offer some familiar moves, a design that suggests that it has not quite detached itself: it begins with something like a claim; it imagines an audience; it sets up criteria for success. ("Floating" may be vague, but the idea does appear to encourage a distinction between an effective and an ineffective paper boat.) In addition, Haynes reassures her readers that her "unrhetoric" would neither "diminish the urgency of teaching students the *relation* of language to decision-making, nor would it circumvent the necessity of teaching rhetoric in the interest of resolving problems" (714). Haynes's unrhetoric remains a pragmatic art: we might eschew the familiar "problem/solution" paper, but we would encourage students to promote "a course of action through writing" (715). We would discourage "taking a position" and instead speak of "*testing contra-distinctions*" (715), suggesting that we are simply asking students to deliberate among alternatives and then to advocate for their choice. In spite of the strangeness of her example assignment, Haynes defends it by appealing to widely held assumptions about the nature and use of rhetoric.

In spite of these small nitpicks, Haynes's idea does push students to think about writing in a new way. It is hard to imagine students reading the assignment sheet and saying, "Oh God, not *this* again." More important, I think, is the assignment's place in her argument. I mean its literal place—namely, the 19th and final endnote of a 57-page article. Why does this placement matter? Because it reflects a basic—and, I would suggest, inescapable—difficulty for postpedagogy: how can we dismantle pedagogy without replacing it with something that might look quite a lot like pedagogy? "It may be time," writes Diane Davis, "to stop offering *more* pedagogy or *altered* pedagogy in answer to the failure of pedagogy" (213). Thus is Haynes's lone suggestion for a practical idea hidden in the 19th endnote. One can understand her hesitation. There is always the risk of the recipe-swap tendency: "I did such-and-such" followed by "Oh, I have to try that!" In her own postpedagogical offering, Sarah J. Arroyo puts it in blunt terms: "Readers may ask how I have specifically practiced what I have been advocating, and may even expect such a description in this final section. However, if I describe a course I have taught and the particular work students produced, I would be implicitly relying on the very assumptions I have critiqued" (706–7). This disclaimer, which seems to see any attempt to intellectualize lore as hopelessly modernist, also appears at the end of Arroyo's article, just at the moment when an impatient reader might wonder, "How am I supposed to *do* this?"

Ultimately, I mean to dispute the assumption—articulated here by Arroyo—that adding to the House of Lore can only ever be interpreted as an attempt to fashion a process. For the moment, however, I submit that Haynes, Davis, and Arroyo are right to worry about offering any new intervention that could be misinterpreted as "the" or even "a" pedagogy. Haynes tries to evade this problem through an assignment that threatens much of the pedagogical apparatus. What is this assignment trying to accomplish? What is its genre? How am I to evaluate it? In designing an assignment that challenges these questions, Haynes also challenges the idea that pedagogy is a corrective to pedagogy. Postpedagogy places its deepest hope in this very challenge. When Thomas Kent writes that writing cannot be taught, and Victor Vitanza that writing should not be taught, when Sidney Dobrin pleads, "Stop talking about teaching" (*Postcomposition* 190), they are all attempting to evade the Monday morning trap ("How am I supposed to *do* this?"). Rather than answering the question, they would undermine the assumptions that the question implies.

Yet this disruptive approach occasions other problems. How, for example, do we resist pedagogy without becoming *anti*-pedagogy and thereby participating in a self-defeating dialectic? To be "anti-pedagogy" is to allow the pedagogical imperative to shape the contours of the argument. This is a familiar claim about binaries: reversing them does not undermine them. In the Hegelian framework, argues John Muckelbauer, "transformation becomes the condition of stability" (10). *Plus ça change . . .* Or, as Kameen puts it,

"The whole notion of a critique that begins with a binary is . . . so poststructuralist that this conversation is going to have to go a long way before it begins to look like an alternative" (103). Indeed, the words *postpedagogy* and *postcomposition* are meant to suggest a paradigm shift (if we still believed in paradigm shifts) in the way we talk about teaching. I read the postpedagogical question in this way: *how do we—can we—talk about teaching without talking about pedagogy?*

To begin answering that question, this chapter examines the postpedagogical argument as it has emerged from both the postprocess articulated by scholars such as Thomas Kent and Gary Olson and third sophistic inquiry articulated by scholars such as Haynes, Arroyo, Lynn Worsham, and Victor Vitanza. I do not pretend to offer anything like a complete examination of the postpedagogical project, but rather to provide an examination of some representative voices within that project.[1] That examination requires a seemingly paradoxical approach that both grants the postpedagogical argument and discerns that argument's limitations. In *Acts of Enjoyment*, Thomas Rickert insists that "to remain vibrant and avoid the rigidity and stagnation common to formulaic approaches" may necessitate "a certain faithlessness to, or even betrayal of . . . founding figures and the grounding concepts they developed" (200). Though I do not adopt Rickert's psychoanalytic frame for my work, his observation suggests the model of argument to which this chapter aspires. I find the postpedagogical argument incredibly compelling, as I hope my initial engagement with Haynes demonstrates. Yet I am also somewhat faithless in that I want to ask "What next?," a question that, at first glance, appears to succumb to the very pedagogical imperative that postpedagogy rejects. The question, then, is whether the "What next?" question can be answered in a way that is consonant with postpedagogical critique. That is the hope of this chapter and the remainder of the book.

OBLIQUE PEDAGOGY

Postpedagogy can be said to emerge largely from the third sophistic school, where the term is most commonly invoked. Yet the basic assumptions can also be found in postprocess theory, a school that emerges more directly as a response to the process paradigm. Therefore, I begin here with postprocess before turning to its third sophistic counterpart. Most readers will be familiar with the basic arguments of postprocess, a theory that, ironically enough, lends itself to poster-ready brevity. Thomas Kent's three-part mantra is well known: "(1) writing is public; (2) writing is interpretive; (3) writing is situated" ("Introduction" 1). With these three claims, Kent means to situate writing so thoroughly in a particular context and moment that "no process can capture what writers do during these changing moments and within these changing relations" (2). Kent (like Victor Vitanza, as we will see in a moment) founds his arguments on Jean-François Lyotard's understanding of *paralogy*, the only approach available after the crisis of legitimation. "We no longer," says Lyotard, "have recourse to the grand narratives—we can resort neither to the dialectic of Spirit nor even to the emancipation of humanity as a validation" (60). Without such overarching validation, or legitimation, we are left with "many different language games—a heterogeneity of elements. They only give rise to institution in patches—local determinism" (xxiv). Patchwork institutions and local determinism cannot offer foundations for grand narratives, including the grand narrative of the writing process. More important, Lyotard sees such language games as unethical. They rely on an "efficiency gained by eliminating, or threatening to eliminate, a player from the language game" (63). Consensus is the problem insofar as it silences dissensus. Paralogy, however, resists this consensus and instead "refines our sensitivity to differences and reinforces our ability to tolerate the incommensurable" (xxv). Paralogy thus describes a sort of attitude toward differences and incommensurability, a refusal to see them as problems to be solved or malfunctions to be corrected. It opens itself to possibilities that cannot be foreseen within grand narratives.

For Kent, the most important aspect of Lyotard's paralogy is that it more accurately depicts our lack of interpretive certainty. Kent thus repurposes paralogy to refer to "the uncodifiable moves we make when we communicate with others, and ontologically, the term describes the unpredictable, elusive, and tenuous decisions or strategies we employ when we actually put language to use" (*Paralogic* 3). Paralogy, Kent goes on to say, "lives beyond logic"; "no logical framework, process, or system can predict in advance the efficacy of our guesses" (*Paralogic* 5). For postprocess, there is no capital *K* Knowledge or capital *T* Theory that can be perceived, described, and repeated regardless of circumstance. "The postmodern critique of theory," writes Gary Olson, "as totalizing and essentialist, and a residue of Enlightenment thinking, has made clear that any attempt to construct a generalizable explanation of how something works is misguided in that such narratives inevitably de-privilege the local, even though it is precisely the local where useful 'knowledge' is generated" ("Toward" 7–8). Without a set of codifiable moves, interpretations have to be made on a case-by-case basis. Put into the terminology of classical rhetoric, postprocess theorists essentially argue that process pedagogy lacks *phronesis*—the kind of practical wisdom associated with situational thinking. As long as process theorists and teachers held to the idea that writing could be depicted in a generalizable explanation, they implicitly rejected the possibility that a writer could make situated, contextual decisions about a particular composition. Process also risks alienating the student, who must conform his or her practices to a set of preset steps. As Joseph Harris observes in *A Teaching Subject*, the drive for a Theory "places some vision of the composing process (rather than an interest in the work of students) at the center of a course in writing" (57). The process thus crowds out even the very students it is meant to serve.

The question of whether postprocess scholars have always described process fairly has been repeatedly debated.[2] But given the way "process" was once a shibboleth in the field, perhaps it is not surprising that postprocess has been so unrelenting in its depiction. John Clifford captures the problem: "As process became more institutionally acceptable and entrenched[,] . . . the progressive engine that powered process in the first place slowed down. Process no longer seemed a more democratic way to know, but simply a technique, a way to proceed, ten steps toward more effective writing, as easily adaptable to teaching executives at IBM as [to] basic writers in South Brooklyn" (Clifford and Ervin 182). Collin Gifford Brooke offers a more succinct view: "Lather. Rinse. Repeat. Freewrite. Write. Rewrite" (qtd. in Voss and Keene 249). Given this reductive uniformity, the zeal to reject process as "processed" is understandable.[3]

What does this rejection mean for pedagogy? Postprocess has offered two answers to this question: everything and nothing. Some argue that postprocess fundamentally undermines our familiar notions of what it means to teach writing and even to be "in" the field of composition. Others argue that postprocess does nothing to change the basic moves of pedagogical practice. Kent belongs to the former camp, insisting bluntly in *Paralogic Rhetoric* that it is impossible to teach writing at all:

> If we accept these claims [that writing and interpretation of writing cannot be codified] we cannot ignore the pedagogical consequence of our position: writing and reading—conceived broadly as processes of knowledge—cannot be taught, for nothing exists to teach. In order to be understood on this point, I need to repeat the commonsense observation that certain background skills, such as an understanding of grammar, can be taught, but the acquisition of these skills never guarantees that a student will be able to communicate effectively; no framework theory of any kind can help a student predict in advance the interpretation that someone else may give an utterance. (161)[4]

For some, Kent's conclusions offer a new understanding of composition itself. Joseph Petraglia argues that postprocess "moved away from the old social scientific assumption that the purpose of research is to intervene and to manipulate. For the writing field, so bound up in *techne* and pedagogy, this might come as distressing news" (60). This is the same observation Vitanza makes about the field of composition. Moreover, Petraglia, like Vitanza, welcomes the possibility that the end of process will expand the reach of the field and its interest in the general, wider ecology of writing itself (63).

Olson sees a similar opportunity: "That the vocabulary of process is no longer useful is not a reason to despair; it is, rather, an invitation to rethink many of our most cherished assumptions about the activity we call 'writing'" ("Toward" 9). Dobrin agrees that the field is now too complex to "rely on a single theory or comprehensive pedagogy to answer all the questions that arise in classrooms or in scholarly inquiry as to the nature of discourse" (*Constructing* 150). Like Petraglia and Olson, Dobrin hopes to move composition's discourse far beyond the pedagogical. In their introduction to 2011's *Beyond Postprocess*, Dobrin and his coauthors emphasize postprocess's "unapologetic resistance to simple pedagogical application" (3). They do not address whether complex application is possible but instead assert that the discipline's view of pedagogy has always been shaped by the assumption that "a subject can be given access to codifiable processes that lend to the production of written text" (13). Their emphasis is entirely in keeping with postpedagogy's desire for disruption. They seek a "disciplinary disruptive maneuver," "disciplinary and institutional critique," and "disciplinary violence" (14) against composition's "disciplinary pedagogical dictate" (17). It is not composition per se that is the problem; it is composition conceived as a teaching subject.[5]

At the same time, some postprocess thinkers have argued that, while the theory may undermine pedagogy as we normally understand it, it does not undermine teaching itself. Bruce McComiskey argues that "the 'post' in postprocess should not represent a radical break with the composing process movement" (40). Rather than seeing postprocess as a rupture or a rejection of process, McComiskey sees it simply as an "extension into the social world of discourse" (41). Others have gone even further in their moderation. Olson argues that we have never really *taught* students to write at all. That does not mean, however, that students cannot *learn* to write. In the end, postprocess involves no major change in what we do in the classroom: "Of course we'll show them ways to prewrite and organize and revise and copyedit and proofread and collaborate. Of course we'll engage in group work and collaborative activities of various kinds. Nothing pedagogically has changed.

What changes is your own understanding of what you are doing in the classroom" ("Why?" 427). Petraglia also sounds reassuring: "Of course, the fundamental observation that an individual produces text by means of a writing process has not been discarded. Instead, it has dissolved and shifted from figure to ground" (53). These reassurances have occasioned the objection that postprocess has not gone far enough. Collin Brooke and Thomas Rickert complain, "Both process and postprocess theories rely on essentially humanist assumptions about what writing is, how it occurs, how it is received, and how it is taught" (163). To spend time worrying about whether writing can be taught "at a time when the activity itself is radically changing, seems especially problematic, like moving deck chairs on the *Titanic*" (163). Raúl Sánchez joins Brooke and Rickert in their skepticism about postprocess: "Both [process and postprocess] work well within composition studies' established disposition toward theory, which is to treat it as a service component of the teaching project at the field's core" ("First" 191). Theory serves first and foremost to inform and reshape our teaching, and postprocess has not managed to escape this orbit.

Perhaps the most famous member of the "don't worry, be happy" school of postmodern pedagogy is Stanley Fish. Though Fish's pedagogical arguments predate postprocess thinking, they grow from the same anti-foundationalist soil.[6] "A situation," he writes, "is always on the wing, and any attempt to capture it will only succeed in fixing it in a shape it no longer has" ("Anti-Foundationalism" 352). Yet affirming this basic tenet of postprocess theory avails us nothing because "composition teachers are always teaching situations because they can do nothing else" (352). If we agree that all knowledge is situated, then even that claim itself is situated. As such, it cannot be abstracted into a claim that can do us any good in any other situation. Lest this seem disturbing to compositionists, Fish assures us that there is no reason to fret: "This leaves me and you only a few worn and familiar bromides: practice makes perfect, you learn to write by writing, you must build on what you already know; but anti-foundationalism tells us that these bromides are enough, tells us that as situated beings our practice can make perfect, and that we already know more than we think" (355). Fish does not explore how these observations can be extracted from situations and shaped into bromides, which would seem to violate the most important claims of his argument and his assertion that he has "nothing to sell" (355).[7] His ultimate point, however, is that composition does not need to buy anything.

The only hope left, writes Kent, lies in an indirect approach to teaching in which teachers "become co-workers who actively collaborate with their students to help them through different communicative situations both within and outside the university" (*Paralogic* 166). In effect, postprocess offers an oblique pedagogy, one whose gaze is not squared firmly on its object. We can expose students to new situations, but that is all we can do. We cannot know ahead of time what students will learn from those situations, nor can we say what they will take from those situations into other situations. "This is exactly," writes Olson, "what postprocess says. It says that writing is a supremely *rhetorical* activity. It arises from the exact purpose of the writer in the exact context of the writing" ("Why?" 426).[8] By offering new contexts, a teacher does not teach students to write in a conventional educational sense of transferring portable information. What we are left with, then, is the fundamental problem of teaching for uncertainty. If we could teach it, it would not be uncertainty. *Contra* Fish, this is no small idea, since, as Olson suggests, it irrevocably changes the way we understand our own work. Yet aside from a few pages in Kent's *Paralogic Rhetoric*, postprocess has not imagined what that changed understanding might look like. It is easier and blunter simply to say, "Don't talk about teaching." That exhortation makes the anti-logical, dialectical assumption that speaking about pedagogy must equal speaking about process. We are to stop talking about teaching because we seem to make the same mistake every time. There is something to this argument: composition's experiences with process and with theory should indeed humble our pedagogical conversation. But need those experiences end it?

PIERCING PEDAGOGIES

Throughout the third sophistic canon, one finds a unifying thread, which can perhaps be best summed up with a Vitanzan sound bite: "*Programs lead to Pogroms!* Therefore, Diaspora! Diaspora! Diaspora forever*" ("Concerning" 417). This claim animates the entire third sophistic school.[9] We can see it, for example, in Haynes's exhortation to consider ourselves refugees, people in flight from sovereignties rather than revolutionaries overthrowing them. We can see it as well in Diane Davis's celebration of laughter and Thomas Rickert's endorsement of *jouissance* and enjoyment. We can even see it in Byron Hawk's attempt to rescue method from its modernist tendencies in his *Counter-History*. The third sophistic school is marked first and foremost by this skepticism about programs, which, the argument goes, inevitably lead to exclusion and suppression. All of these writers are skittish about composition's will-to-control, even when the politics on offer may be more to our liking. In Lyotard's terms, even a "right-minded" program insists on consensus around a single language game, and anyone who wants to play the game differently, or to play a different game, is out of luck. If the question is pedagogy, the third sophistic school worries that any new pedagogical game will eventually silence even newer ones. The idea is not to build a better mousetrap but to stop building such traps altogether. Therefore, even the postprocess answer may seem too conservative. Rather than paralogic interpretation, third sophistic is most interested in paralogic invention, which will not manage utterances already made but rather produce utterances not yet made or even imagined. Rather than the hermeneutic guesswork and "successful" communication offered by Kent, the third sophistic school seeks invention that reconfigures the very idea of success.

The third sophistic starts with Vitanza, who casts himself as composition's court jester, mocking our will-to-disciplinarity and our desire to be taken seriously by our peers in the university. Vitanza does not see the history of rhetoric as foundational material for a "serious" university discipline; instead, he sees anti-foundational provocations toward ongoing perversities. "I *exhort,*" he says, "*as a Pragmatic (Sophistic) Provocateur,* in jest, as a fool subversively jests before *The Court of Aristotelian philosophical Rhetoric,* a diseased Court with a Rhetoric that has far too much feudal power and that needs (ought) to be overthrown" ("Critical" 57). Vitanza's target here is what we might call "normal" historiography, the sort that tries to build up a grand narrative—in this case, a coherent tradition of rhetorical progress. But *consensus, coherent,* and *progress* are all devil terms that threaten to suppress voices and rhetorics that might muss our tidy house. Vitanza's historiography, on the other hand, is "not concerned either with attempting to resolve rhetorical, interpretive differences or with even accounting for them. Instead, it identifies, detonates, and exploits the differences" ("Critical" 42). If the rhetorical tradition offers a Cicero, Vitanza would offer the second sophistic; if it offers Erasmus, he would offer Montaigne. For him, the great Roman poet is not Virgil, but Ovid, who wrote not imperial epic but scandalous lyric.

Yet Vitanza would play the counterstatement game only until someone suggested a counterreformation. At that moment and in that move, Vitanza sees potential for nothing but another kind of consensus, another kind of coherence: "to speak of 'revolution' is always simultaneously to speak of the Law. Or, put another way: to be sub/versive of the Law is still at once to be 'subject' to the Law" ("Concerning" 397). As long as rhetoric plays the game of philosophy's "law," it will still be caught in philosophy's dialectic. Like Kent, Vitanza would instead play a game of paralogy, a game that would "bear witness to the unintelligible or to disputes or differences of opinion that are systematically disallowed by the dominant language game of homological science and are therefore 'silenced'" ("Three" 146). Paralogy is a latter-day sophistic that seeks "not only to make the weaker argument the stronger but also to favor a radical heterogeneity of discourses over either the favored protocol of One or the homogeneity of the Many" ("Three" 147). To avoid these dialectical traps, Vitanza urges us toward "illegitimate couplings!" (*Negation* 5). Or, in a mantra-like intonation, "Just link. Just link. Just link" (*Negation* 5). Following Lyotard, Vitanza sees rhetoric as an activity not of the *polis* but of the *pagus,* "not a sentimentalized, romanticized, Rousseauistic country" but a "wild, savage . . . country. If any country at all. It is an *atopos* of Third subject/object, Sophistic positions-that-are-not-positions" (*Negation* 51–52). Vitanza's nonpositional, paralogic "unstance" offers a "nondisciplinary" rhetoric that is not concerned with answering a certain kind of philosophic demand for serious consideration. At this point, Vitanza senses that many of his readers might be losing patience with his sophistic shifting: "And so, *You*, my (bourgeois!?) readers—perhaps out of frustration?—now, if not previously, ask: 'What's really the bottom line here?' 'Our' (scrambled) response: there's no bottom and, of course, no official 'line' other than countless *ad hoc* 'lines of flight'" ("Concerning" 408–9).

What does this mean for pedagogy? For Vitanza, that is the wrong question. In fact, it begs the question. Teaching, as it is usually understood, is the very modernist enterprise that Vitanza would overthrow: "Can anyone of my (even more open-minded) readers, therefore, imagine the National Council of Teachers of English [NCTE] or the College Composition and Communication Conference [CCCC] having as its conference theme the question Should writing be taught?" ("Three" 161). As Vitanza suggests, this sophistic game may not be welcome in a discipline centering its legitimacy on the teaching of writing. "This [paralogic] conclusion, to be sure, is and will not be a popular one, since it would entail, for instance, a 'post-pedagogy' for, or a non-Platonic and non-Aristotelian approach to, composition theory that would *dramatically change* the activity we call teaching" ("Critical" 43–44). Here, we find one of the first invocations of postpedagogy in composition, in this case as a rejection of the lingering Platonic/Aristotelian dream. Vitanza explicates that vision in "Three Countertheses," which appeared in the now-seminal *Contending with Words* (Harkin and Schilb) in 1991. Founded on Gorgias's three-part "On the Nonexistent," Vitanza's argument seeks to challenge the "strong *will* of the field of composition; . . . (1) the will to systematize (the) language (of composing), (2) the will to be its author(ity), and (3) the will to teach it to students" ("Three" 140). Against these wills to system, authority, and pedagogy, Vitanza offers his own countertheses. The first rejects the idea of a universal foundation because "it does not emancipate but only enslaves and impoverishes us" ("Three" 146). The second counterthesis is a mirror of the first. Just as there are no grand narratives, there is no single, unified "self" who speaks or writes discourse. Once again, Vitanza locates his understanding of this idea in Lyotard's notion of language games. Composition, he suggests, tends to play one of two games, in which either the writer controls language or the reader is controlled by language. Vitanza rejects these in favor of Lyotard's paralogic listening game ("Three" 152–53). Positioned as a listener, the speaker or writer cannot become the authority who subjects listeners and readers to language. In Gorgian terms, even if something exists (to teach), it cannot be known (because "knowing" plays the language game that subjects language to the writer).

Finally, and most important for the present argument, the third counterthesis forwards the postpedagogical project by stating that even if something can be known, it should not be taught, since teaching it would inevitably require reducing it. Theory, Vitanza writes, "finally resists being theorized" ("Three" 159). This claim leads to the moratorium on turning theory into practice or pedagogy, along with the suggestion that CCCC should consider the question of whether writing should even be taught. This final counterthesis most directly addresses composition's investment in pedagogy, an investment that Vitanza would like us to withdraw. "What we want, then, is a *pedagogy other(wise)*" (161), or what he later calls "a way to proceed without foundations and without criteria (the first counterthesis) and without knowing as a subject (the second) and without conventional theory and pedagogy (the third). What we want, then, is . . . a paralogic pedagogy" (165). He urges composition to discard the Socratic cast of traditional *paideia,* which insists on certain criteria of knowledge—that it can be codified, reproduced, and therefore taught. To know in Socratic dialectic is to "systematize ambiguity" (163). Anything that cannot be assimilated to such a system is denied the status of knowledge. Vitanza would rather dwell in ambiguity, and he assures the reader that "there are precedents aplenty" if we are looking for the sort of "counterstrategies" to which he is alluding: Lyotard, Deleuze and

Guattari, Derrida, Barthes, Feyerabend (165). While composition should not aspire to theoretical grounds for a new and improved system, it can turn to such theorists for strategies with which to resist pedagogy. *Paralogic pedagogy* remains a contradiction in terms insofar as paralogy does not seek "a" new pedagogy that will authorize a discipline. "For paralogy, the goal is not renovation but innovation; not a stochastic series based on rules that allow us to guess effectively and efficiently but a paradoxical series that invites us to break with the former rules altogether" (166). Here, we see the fundamental difference between Kent's postprocess and Vitanza's postpedagogy. Vitanza is not interested in a hermeneutics, not even in stochastic rules that might produce better guesses about other people's meaning. Paralogy, Vitanza suggests, does not help us produce passing theories, which seems too cautious a goal; rather, it offers links that reconfigure the familiar into the unfamiliar.

Yet Vitanza also seems aware of the difficulty of maintaining a paradoxical, paralogic approach to invention. "It may very well be, however, that we cannot avoid Programmatic Thinking! (The body-hysteric is weak!) Therefore, we must ever be suspicious. (We must ever be on the move, ever *drift*, be forever *nomadic*.)" ("Concerning" 417). This is the same attitude exemplified in Haynes's "Writing Offshore." By casting ourselves adrift, we can perhaps cut ourselves loose from the programmatic habit. Vitanza would also not be read as suggesting that we *ought* to follow his lead. If his exhortation to suspicion seems like the precise hermeneutics animating "critical pedagogy," he also insists that his call is "simultaneously *not* a call" for any disciplinary change in direction; if James Berlin says he cannot do what Vitanza does, Vitanza says that he never asked Berlin to be different in any way: "I-cum-we, instead, need them to do as they do" (417). The sophists need Socrates as badly as Socrates needs the sophists. What would a paradoxical series of rules do without a former set of rules from which to break?

In asking this question, I fear that I sound like a resentful Apollonian: "It's all very well for you to have your Dionysian debauch out there in the *pagus*, but while you're out drinking, *someone* has got to maintain the temples back here in the *polis*." I'm worrying about adopting the ethos of the Prodigal Son's older brother, who has only enough virtue to complain that he gets no credit for being virtuous. I realize that my question is fueled by the very dialectic that Vitanza would cast down. Yet his argument seems unavoidably to suggest that there must always be a set of old rules or conventional thinking or standard pedagogy that we can target. In other words, the most difficult question occasioned by Vitanza's work is this: should pedagogy seek to inspire student resistance to itself? The problem with critical pedagogy may well be that it seeks to encourage resistance explicitly. It says, without irony, that the student will be rewarded for complying with the teacher's request to resist the targets the teacher chooses. Vitanza, however, would seem to prefer that pedagogy itself become a target of resistance. If that is the case, is it our role as teachers to point to the target or to provide it? How do we inhabit a role through which we encourage resistance to the very workings of what we do?

This problem continues to challenge the postpedagogical project, as we can see in some of the thought that Vitanza has inspired. Take, for example, Diane Davis's *Breaking Up [at] Totality: A Rhetoric of Laughter*. Like Vitanza, Davis laments the fact that composition has "not allowed what Lyotard calls 'the postmodern condition' to radically refashion our pedagogical goals" (6). The changes we have made—collaborative learning, personal expression, even the acknowledgment of process itself—have not pried us away from writing the same kinds of texts as we always have. Davis tries not only to persuade her readers of these claims but also to enact and embody the rhetorical values she articulates. As she writes, she does not want to "'argue well' but rather to *write differently*, to make an/other kind of sense. This text [her own] will be less interested in proving a(ny) point than in inviting unusual linkages, in calling for new idioms, in holding the space of questioning open" (5). On the actual printed page, this sentence is visually interrupted by this block quote: "EXPECT SOME LEAKSsss." Thus does the book's design mirror its purpose, which is to "break up what is called 'composition' by engaging in third sophistic rereadings of the grounds upon which this 'discipline' has been built" (7). We will break up the discipline, she writes, "*by inviting in everybody*" (7) and by allowing for the "excess" and "overflow" of experience, reaction, and thought that cannot be contained within the rational or the planned. Like the suppressed laughter that strikes us in spite of ourselves, the "laughter" Davis wants to hear would disrupt the usual modernist program of rhetoric and composition (21–22). If you believe that we are used by language as much as we use language, then humanist pedagogy becomes a Procrustean bed for which the actual human has to be distorted to fit. Instead, Davis would have a Protean pedagogy, one that is shifting, surprising, and unpredictable.

But a Protean pedagogy, like a paralogic pedagogy, seems a contradiction in terms. It cannot be manifest in a pogrom-inducing program. A revised pedagogy, according to Davis, would simply reenact the same modernist or Enlightenment assumption that the right pedagogical system can produce the right kind of subject and the right sort (i.e., *our* sort) of person. Following Vitanza's critique of Berlin, Davis's critique targets not just current traditional pedagogy but also feminist and critical pedagogy. The former wants someone ready to produce within the framework of late capitalism; the latter wants someone to critique the framework of late capitalism. Either way, the student is marching under someone else's orders. "Even so-called emancipatory pedagogical techniques function within a disciplinary matrix of power. . . . Inasmuch as these pedagogies are pledged at some level to the grand narrative of emancipation and to the mobilization of the Grand March, they participate in the carceral network they so desperately hope to transcend" (212). The "liberatory" pedagogies the field has produced have succeeded only in rebuilding pedagogy's prison house. A new pedagogy cannot be the solution, because the problem of pedagogy is pedagogy itself. "It may be time," therefore, "to stop offering *more* pedagogy or *altered* pedagogy in answer to the failure of pedagogy" (213). As with postprocess, the very terms of Davis's argument preclude her from offering a replacement: "We're not talking about a face lift for composition instruction; we're talking about a radical rrrr-u-p-t-u-r-e of what we thought was possible" (247).

This is her pedagogy of laughter, which seeks "moments, instances, glimpses, flashes. We are after an instantaneous gestalt switch rather than a long-term political program; *we are after tactics rather than strategies*" (56; emphasis added). *Tactics rather than strategies* provides a fitting complement to *Programs lead to pogroms*. This kind of ad hoc reaction is contained in Davis's very title: "breaking up [at] totality." Alternative pedagogies "enter the fight" and "therefore assume the rules of that fight and end up protecting and perpetuating rather than dethroning" (211). In contrast to this mistake, the only thing Davis can encourage is rupture/disruption/interruption, beyond the teacher's control.

But this rhetoric of comedy leaves us with a question: should teachers be in on the joke or play the straight man? Consider Davis's representative anecdote about a time from her childhood when she tried not to giggle during church. The preacher had a loose strand of hair floating off the back of his head, and its movement betrayed the seriousness of his conscious rhetorical performance. Davis could barely contain herself. In this story, the minister (i.e., the teacher) is not in on the joke; he is the joke. He is not the jester, but the butt. It seems, then, that this pedagogy is laughing at you rather than laughing with you. I do not raise this question to protect my dignity but rather to discover how one offers pedagogy itself as an object of critique without reinscribing the very logic of liberatory pedagogy. The basic question of critical pedagogy is whether the teacher can ever escape her authoritative role, and the rhetoric of laughter seeks not to solve this problem but to disrupt its movement. That disruption, however, does not really address the question of the teacher's role. If we are to get out of the business of cultivating subjectivities, should we be the students' collaborators in their more independent subject formation, or should we be their opponents in order to spark that formation? If the answer is the latter, then should we conclude that it would be better to reinstitute conventional forms of authority that might occasion resistance by being oppressive? Should we impose totalities for students to break up (at)? If, on the other hand, we decide to encourage the rhetoric of laughter, it loses its disruptive potential. We are back to where we started.

We see the same catch-22 in other postpedagogical arguments, such as Thomas Rickert's *Acts of Enjoyment*. Like Vitanza and Davis, Rickert is suspicious of critical pedagogies—particularly the cultural studies brand—that claim to liberate students from false ideology. Rickert worries that critical pedagogy, as it is currently practiced, will fail and will therefore simply encourage cynicism in his students (1–2). While he does not reject the basic desires of James Berlin's critical project, he nevertheless worries that Berlin's method is no longer sufficient to the moment. Rickert's students may be able to take apart an advertisement for designer jeans, but that does not stop them from purchasing the jeans (1–2). Rickert thus faces the familiar challenge of hatching a pedagogy that will not simply impose upon students a different set of political beliefs. "The question is simultaneously a practical one—what can we do to produce better citizens and rhetors?—and a theoretical one—can we develop rhetorical theories that surmount the insufficiencies of contemporary cultural studies?" (3). For Rickert, the understanding of the human person provided by Lacanian and Zizekian thought lays the groundwork for a different approach, one predicated on accepting *jouissance* as a fundamental part of human experience. Rickert defines *jouissance* as the "largely unconscious enjoyment one derives from habits, attitudes, beliefs and activities" (3). Critique itself can be an enjoyable habit whether or not it results in real change. Unless cultural studies can account for this unconscious enjoyment—and unless it can resist the urge to label some enjoyments as politically unsound—it cannot hope to succeed in its project of ideological transformation.[10]

When he turns to the book's pedagogical chapter, Rickert examines what may be the most infamous essay ever produced in a composition course: the Quentin Pierce piece described in David Bartholomae's "Tidy House." In response to an assignment on Sartre, Pierce submits a piece of writing that seems to reject not only the assignment but also the very premises of education. At first glance, the paper appears to say, "Fuck this and fuck you." This baffles Bartholomae: "I was not prepared for this paper. In a sense, I did not know how to read it. I could only ignore it" (6). Bartholomae recognizes that the paper evidences rhetorical skill: the author has sized up the situation and his audience (in this case, Bartholomae) and has correctly concluded what Bartholomae himself admits: that the assignment is part of a curriculum "that spent 14 weeks slowly and inevitably demonstrating [students'] failures" (5). Pierce's response thus indicates a great deal of insight and, even more important, integrity. At the very least, it risks something greater than the accepted response: "'In this fast-paced modern world, when one considers the problems facing mankind . . .' I know you know how to imagine and finish that essay. It has none of the surprises of the fuck you essay" (7). For Rickert, as for Bartholomae, Pierce's essay presents a serious problem for the teacher. On the one hand, it would undermine Pierce's transgression to somehow "accommodate" his writing by rewarding it in any way. There would be nothing worse than telling him, "Hey, man, I *hear* you." On the other hand, to dismiss Pierce's writing as a violation of expectation would simply confirm his suspicions: my writing is meaningless because even this thumb-in-the-eye cannot upset the usual economy of expectation.

Rickert would avoid both of these outcomes, and he interprets Pierce's writing as a transgression against the either-or interpretive structure that does not know what to do with it in the first place. Rickert calls the essay an "Act," a piece that "is interested in disrupting the day, in transforming the entire discursive field that determines what is proper and valued" (*Acts* 194). Thus, this particular Act "works" insofar as it haunts the teacher whose assignment encouraged it. Among the values it disrupts are the basic pedagogical values of prediction and control: "If you do this, then this will happen; if you plan ahead, you will save time; if you are critical of power, you will be empowered" (194). The Act rejects this logic even at the risk of a loss of control, or de-Oedipalization. But Rickert also insists that the Act can push beyond a simple, reactive re-Oedipalization (i.e., "fuck you, *too*") in favor of *post*-Oedipalization, which "would refuse the reproduction of the everyday, or, better, seek to reenchant the everyday via the new, the unthought, the unaccommodatable" (195). The Act does not replace

one set of available means with another. Instead, it offers the unavailable means. Our task, according to Rickert, is to prepare ourselves to respond to such work, to avoid the alternatives of either
condescending to it or burying it in a drawer for twenty years.
Once we find ourselves as upset as Pierce, it is our responsibility to
discern our own position in the new economy of expectation he has
managed to create.

Reading this piece, Rickert's most important conclusion is
postpedagogical in a somewhat literal sense: "Any writing pedagogy that could learn from Pierce's Act would have to accept in
advance that pedagogy cannot be orchestrated directly to produce
forms of writing that would be Acts. To do so would be to rein-
scribe the pedagogical fantasy of control" (*Acts* 195). "Advance(d)
pedagogy," so to speak, remains impossible, and "the pedagogy of
the unexpected" remains a contradiction in terms. To imagine that
pedagogy can lead to some particular outcome is to "stumble upon
the core fantasy underpinning rhetoric: the phantasmic assumption
that our intentions have the desired effects for the reasons we think
they do" (206). The work of postpedagogy is at its heart an attempt
to disrupt this fantasy. Postpedagogy positions the teacher less as
the cause of the Act and more as its effect. It offers "an exhortation
to dare, to invent, to create, to risk. It is less a body of rules, a set of
codifiable classroom strategies, than a willingness to give recognition and value to unorthodox, unexpected, or troublesome work"
(196). The only thing we can do ahead of time is to encourage our
students toward the new and the unthought; then we must wait and
be ready to respond to both when they emerge. This position, of
course, demands that Rickert avoid prescribing—or proscribing—
any classroom practice. But that does not mean we need be frozen
with trepidation, unable to imagine any intervention. During the
"pedagogy wars of the 1990s," he argues, "one risked terrible damage to students in choosing the 'wrong' pedagogy" (207). Rickert
would seem to have us question this basic presumption, suggesting
that pedagogies do far less damage (or, perhaps, good?) than we
think. More crucial is the way we approach our classrooms: "The
performative and symbolic aspects of pedagogy are as important,

if not sometimes more so, than the specific content" (207). The basic line of liberatory pedagogy is not its content or goal but its own authoritarian streak. As with Davis's rhetoric of laughter, the issue then becomes how we inhabit our role as teachers, in which we cannot escape authority, without also becoming authoritarian. Rickert's emphasis therefore falls naturally not on how we "front-load" the classroom but rather on what comes off the back end. The teacher is positioned as a receptor of Acts rather than as their producer.

Yet the traditional question of pedagogy—namely, how do we occasion the kind of student writing we would prefer to see—does not go entirely unaddressed: "Ultimately writing the Act, *or a pedagogy that would create the conditions of possibility for Acts*, must abandon the drive for explanations that would control and codify what is written and abandon the attendant faith that is placed in these explanations" (Rickert, *Acts* 197; emphasis added). I do not want to make too much of a single phrase in a 200-page book, but a lot hangs on the idea of Act-friendly conditions. In spite of his reassurances that we not worry too much about the "wrong" pedagogy, Rickert here implies that one can imagine a pedagogy that is more likely to produce what we want. Certainly, there is an appreciable distance between a pedagogy that guarantees outcomes and a pedagogy content with the possibility of certain outcomes. If we admit the latter possibility, we have not entirely escaped the question of pedagogy. Lest we worry that we might create the wrong conditions, Rickert assures us again: "We might aspire to see how these 'Act-ive' moments are already present in student writing in countless different ways, making classroom practices a forum for lighting up the thousand tiny resistances that irrepressibly emerge" and "that can offer so much to revitalize pedagogical work" (197–98). It is even less clear, then, that our pedagogical choices matter at all. Whether we create the conditions or not, "Act-ive" resistance will occur. As with Davis's pedagogy of laughter, we are left wondering whether we should encourage Acts or attempt to suppress them in the hope of smoking them out. Pierce's Act, after all, was occasioned by a really bad assignment and a really bad pedagogy, a course that, Bartholomae admits, just about guaranteed the failure of most of the students in the class (7). Surely it would be pedagogical malpractice to invite an Act by knowingly operating out of such a curriculum.

In making these observations, I do not mean to dismiss Rickert's visions of the postpedagogical project. I agree it would revitalize pedagogical work to see it as literally postpedagogical—that is, as something that follows the production of writing rather than preceding it. My project is also consonant with those of Davis and Rickert insofar as we believe that changing teaching first requires a change in the way teachers position themselves and then a change in the way they position students. If we are concerned about subjectivities, we might start with our own and ask whether we are as subject to our students' inscription as they are to ours. Yet even if we want to emphasize the way we respond to student writing, it seems to me that we cannot evade the obligation to consider the ways in which we occasion student writing. Outcomes may not be susceptible to guarantee, but they still bear some relation to inputs. Composition, to be sure, has concentrated so much thought on the pedagogy of occasion that it is refreshing, if nothing else, to shift our emphasis to a pedagogy of response. But we still must consider how we and our students are subject to our pedagogical design.

Given this necessity, Davis's and Rickert's arguments leave us with unpleasant choices. There is what I have been calling the straight-man choice, in which our course, like the one Bartholomae describes, might offer a sort of reverse psychology. If that seems too nefarious, we are told not to worry, since resistance will happen no matter what we do.[11] Why, then, speak of creating the conditions for Acts at all? Indeed, these arguments suggest that is the precise question we should *not* answer precisely because it invites the usual fantasy of control. And yet it seems insupportable that we would simply do whatever and wait to see what might happen. Rickert would likely insist that he is advocating no such thing. His psychoanalytic approach would "provide us with . . . vocabularies, theories, and insights that can aid us in expanding, honing, or otherwise further developing whatever we are working with" (*Acts*

207). This stance does not mean that we must settle on *a* pedagogy or reignite any wars over *the* pedagogy, but it does suggest that our choices matter, that we can make bad choices as well as good ones. The problem of discerning the difference between the two remains. How do we know when our teaching habits, attitudes, beliefs, and activities have become arresting rather than generative? (Or when it's time to be arresting rather than generative?) How do we maintain what Burke might call a "liquid attitude" toward our teaching (*Attitudes* 231)?

While few postpedagogues would call themselves Burkeans, a liquid attitude appears to be what they are after. I am not sure, however, that they finally articulate a way to maintain such an attitude. To put this another way: When I'm asking about the sustainability of postpedagogy, I do not mean to ask how it can be turned into a program. I mean to ask how I can inhabit the attitudes that postpedagogy encourages, given that I am, as Burke would say, rotten with perfection and goaded by the spirit of hierarchy ("Definition"). Rickert tells us that *jouissance* "makes everything we do worthwhile, yet it also makes us less amenable to change than most rhetorical theories of persuasion would have us believe" (*Acts* 20). As I understand it, then, *jouissance* is why I enjoy teaching, but it also may be why I enjoy habits or attitudes that arrest my own and my students' growth rather than encouraging it. Since *jouissance* is not entirely susceptible to conscious intervention, perhaps the best I or anyone can do is to maintain a liquid attitude. Maintaining that attitude does require some intervention, some habit of thought that keeps us from being too deeply in love with our own enjoyment. In the postpedagogical school, the most plausible intervention is offered by Byron Hawk, to whom I turn in the next and final section.

METHODICAL PEDAGOGY

Byron Hawk's *A Counter-History of Composition* is unusual in the postpedagogical canon in that it attempts to offer a postpedagogical *method*. In keeping with the spirit of postpedagogy, Hawk's method is not one of pedagogical process so much as pedagogical discernment.

Hawk shares the same postpedagogical perspective on the dangers of process; following Vitanza, he calls it the problem of *law*. Pedagogy cannot rely on law, but neither can it simply oppose law.[12] The law can impose itself so forcefully that it snuffs out the spirit, but rebelling against it simply reconfirms its importance. Hawk is concerned with the former of these two possibilities; he sees the problems of process(ed) pedagogy everywhere he looks. In his discussion of Richard Young's tagmemics and James Berlin's cultural studies, for example, he claims that "the application of a pre-set strategy inevitably becomes law when implemented in the first-year course" (208). Again, this claim is the basis for the entire postpedagogical project. Reading Freire, Hawk insists that the Brazilian educator did not mean for teachers to "turn his pedagogy into law but rather should look to their specific contexts to invent and develop pedagogical practices, processes, and methods" (218). Reading Ira Shor, Hawk concludes that critical pedagogy cannot escape the fact that "teachers are a part of institutional structures, a manifestation of law" and later adds that "liberatory pedagogy tends to sidestep . . . the fact that students can and do see teachers as embodying the power of law" (211). (This is the very same issue we see in Davis's pedagogy of laughter. Shall we occasion laughter, or shall we be its objects?) Hawk's solution to the problem of the law is offered in a Lyotardian and Vitanzan endorsement of "linking over law" (244). This idea of linkage—which might operate outside logic rather than be merely anti-logical—will allow teachers and students to resist the temptation to overthrow one law only to impose their own.

Hawk's counterhistory features a few different culprits, including George Kennedy and (as always in postpedagogy) James Berlin, but the central target is Richard Young and his 1980 "Arts, Crafts, Gifts, and Knacks." Young's purpose in that article is to find a reliable method of invention that is neither purely aleatory nor purely algorithmic; in pursuing this goal, however, Young dismisses romanticism/vitalism as nothing more than the mirror of the "rule-governed procedures" (57).[13] In the new romanticism, Young argues, the writing teacher "is no longer a purveyor of information about the craft of writing but a *designer of occasions* that stimulate the creative process" (55; emphasis added). For Young, this notion is too obscure and fanciful to be much use; for Hawk, it is the description of his own pedagogical method. Hawk argues that, despite his faith in the malleability of heuristics, Young's vision includes no internal mechanism or check that might prevent them from becoming another kind of law. In other words, Hawk worries that heuristics do not offer a way to maintain a liquid attitude. Young's "middle ground option," Hawk writes, "does nothing to keep the application of heuristics from generating what are really just new forms of formalism" (*Counter-History* 28). In effect, Hawk accuses Young of pursuing what Ong might call the "method of method." Indeed, though *Counter-History* does not mention Ramus often, Hawk's version of postpedagogy offers another postpedagogical argument directly with the ghost of Ramus, for whom method "signifies a curriculum subject and, by extension, any treatise (dispute) on any matter" (Ong 248–49). This notion of method—shaped by a deductive notion of law, animated by "a routine of efficiency" (Ong 226)—is what Hawk seeks to challenge.

What separates this challenge from other postpedagogical challenges is that Hawk wants to reclaim "method" for composition. Like Ann Berthoff, Hawk believes that the problem of pedagogy lies not with the idea of method per se, but rather with the way the idea of method is so often understood. His goal is to devise a method responsive to "the conditions of possibility that the material situation sets up" (*Counter-History* 45). The problem with a heuristic approach, argues Hawk, is that it "allows Young to disregard context as the ground of heuristics and to overlook the importance of designing occasions as a predominant aspect of composition pedagogy" (249). Occasion design sees context as central to teaching. But as the phrase suggests, occasion design is interested in what Rickert might call creating the conditions for the possibility of Acts. Not content with conceiving postpedagogy as an act of reception, Hawk's "complex vitalist paradigm" (249) is also willing to articulate it as an act of invention and intervention. When he turns to one of his contemporary exemplars, in this case Paul Kameen, Hawk observes a teacher much like the one Rickert implicitly imagines. In his *Writing/Teaching*, Kameen describes a course that he does not feel qualified to teach (poetry by women of color), and he spends much of the book recounting the ways in which he tries to make his own position in the classroom a subject of examination. Kameen demands of himself precisely what he demands of his students. He demonstrates his own attempt to make connections and links among classroom discussion, assigned texts, student writing, and of course the teacher's own contributions (231). Hawk observes Kameen "opting for silence, listening, letting the students' and his own thoughts tacitly develop out of the local ecology rather than a conscious, predetermined political position" (*Counter-History* 233). Like the "Rickertian" teacher of the "Act," the "Kameenian" teacher hangs back in order to allow students to find their own ways. To borrow a phrase from contemporary politics, the Kameenian teacher "leads from behind" and adopts a "rhetoric of listening," which "means listening to discourses not *for* intent but *with* intent—with the intent to understand not just the claims but the rhetorical negotiations of understanding as well" (Ratcliffe 28). As Kameen himself suggests, "I have learned enough over the years to sometimes just let that happen, to accept and participate in the discussion and the lesson *that the group happens to offer me,* even when it's not the one I had anticipated" (129; emphasis added). Notice here the same pedagogical position featured in Rickert's work. The act of teaching is an act of responding, not of eliciting. It is a different kind of outcomes-based education. The basic move of postpedagogy is this: "Here is a set of texts, theories, arguments, ideas, technologies, contexts, desires, forces, subjectivities: what can the student make of them?" (219). Rather than the banking method, we have the co-op(t) method, in which the students, we hope, co-opt our designs for their own occasions.

Yet that leaves unanswered the question of how we make choices about our designs. Hawk does not duck this question so much as he allows others (including Kameen and Gregory Ulmer) to answer it for him. In turning to exemplars, Hawk hopes to check the will-to-method, a check he does not find in Young's endorsement of heuristics. Kameen (and Ulmer), on the other hand, have no way of knowing ahead of time how pedagogy will turn out. This post hoc pedagogy demands an "element of risk" (216) and a "throw of the dice" (217) by trying to place the teacher's work *within* the classroom ecology rather than outside or prior to it. Indeed, ecology is paramount. Like other postpedagogues, Hawk has his own mantra: "Create Contexts, Not Subjects" (*Counter-History* 249). What attracts him to Kameen's work is that Kameen not only creates a rich context but also subjects himself to it. He is both participant and observer. From this kind of description, Hawk draws his "complex vitalist paradigm" (249), a fidelity to situation that prevents method from becoming the method of method and laws from becoming Law. One cannot simply derive a Kameenian pedagogy, because Kameen's pedagogical articulation is inextricably bound up with a particular classroom ecology. Whatever we learn from Kameen will have to be rearticulated and repurposed for our own situations.

Still, the question for the would-be occasion designer remains: why decide on those exemplars? In asking this question, I do not mean to reject Hawk's choices but rather to observe that he is *making* choices, choices that presuppose a set of values he has brought with him to his classroom work. Pedagogy cannot avoid these values and choices, so it cannot be an entirely *post hoc* activity. Hawk is, of course, aware of this: "In a complex vitalist paradigm, being attentive to the ways we design our constellations and *to the ethical effects they produce* becomes the central pedagogical concern" (*Counter-History* 257; emphasis added). "A complex vitalist hope," he then adds, "would take an active role in designing pedagogical contexts and hope the students come to understand their situatedness and learn to develop ethical connections that lead to productive acts and texts" (258). Like any responsible teacher, Hawk cannot help but come to the classroom with a set of ethical expectations. Perhaps these are not expressed in an overt political ideology, as they are in Berlinian-inflected cultural studies pedagogy, but Hawk implicitly observes the possibility that student Acts—which we now might define in Hawkian terms as the constellation whose connections we did not and could not anticipate—may either confirm or scandalize our notion of the ethical. What is supposed to happen if a student makes a set of "unethical" connections, suggesting that our curriculum had produced a set of "unethical" effects? Obviously, Hawk's judgment of such outcomes depends on the classroom ecology he encounters. But even articulating a notion of "the ethical," as he does in the previous sentences, suggests a set of values that he has brought to the ecology. This is not something he should be embarrassed about; it is not something he can avoid. But it does reveal that even the complex vitalist teacher's discernment depends on judgments that travel from one situation to the next. Otherwise, he would have no means of choosing exemplars like Kameen and Ulmer. Or, following the implications of Davis's and Rickert's arguments, he could choose an obsolete pedagogy and potentially get the same results. Indeed, one of the most profound implications of the postpedagogical argument is that no pedagogy may finally be obsolete, since any pedagogy may well effect a productive classroom ecology.

Let me illustrate my claim with an analogy: Hawk is arguing for a curriculum that resembles the television show *Chopped,* in which contestant chefs are offered a group of seemingly disparate ingredients and asked to make something palatable of them. The chefs cannot ignore any ingredient; their challenge is to make something good out of whatever they are given. Because they are not given recipes to follow, what they produce is their own, even though the materials were chosen for them. When they are judged, it is not against a set standard, since the judges do not know ahead of time what they will produce. Instead, their work is judged against their own intentions—that is, the judges tend to say things like, "I see what you were trying to do here, but I'm not sure you succeeded," or "It seems to me that you were going for A, but I think you've gotten B instead." Of course, the show is a contest, not a classroom, and three rounds of surprise ingredients do not constitute curricular materials. Nevertheless, the show raises questions in my mind that postpedagogy—even in Hawk's methodical articulation—has not quite answered. Clearly, the ingredients on *Chopped* are chosen purposely, with ideas of possible design already in mind. The contestants are given things that might work well together, even though no one yet knows *how* they might work well together. (At the very least, all the items are food.) Moreover, like the complex, vitalist, postpedagogical teacher, *Chopped*'s judges *might be disappointed by what their "students" produce*. Failure is an option. And that is because the postpedagogue has brought some idea of success to the ecology. My point, then, is that Hawk has not been methodical enough. What would make him decide, for example, that a pedagogical intervention had failed? How would he decide on what to keep from a previous ecology and what to throw away? Between the poles of the unattainable ideal and past failure, how do we discern and interpret the precedents on which we would rely for guidance? How, in other words, do we maintain our own liquid attitude toward our ideas of failure and success?

Even if we insist that our pedagogy can be manifest only within particular classroom ecologies, students (and teachers) will arrive in those ecologies having experienced other ecologies. In "Toward the *Chora*: Kristeva, Derrida, and Ulmer on Emplaced Invention," Rickert writes of a novelist "who once responded to the question of whether or not writing novels made it easier to write future novels. The answer was no; the reasons were that every novel required new approaches and solutions to fresh problems that past writing experience could not cover" ("Toward" 263). Not being a novelist, I have little standing to quarrel with a novelist's perception of his or her process. But the statement quarrels with itself. It is only through the experience of writing previous novels that the novelist can say with any authority that experience will be of no help. One cannot deny the usefulness of experience without implying some understanding of that experience in the first place. Of course, we can understand our experience in myriad different ways, and the experience of previous processes for previous projects might convince us that new projects require new processes. But even this negative lesson suggests that we cannot escape our experience. This fact is attested to in Kameen's idea of "ideological autobiography," the personal essays included in *Writing/Teaching* that chronicle his search for his own place in his classroom ecology. In writing these brief memoirs, Kameen tries to locate that place through his own experience—of being a male, a Catholic, an early (and secret) lover of poetry, a student of feminism, a son, a father. If we are to imitate and repurpose pedagogy like Kameen's—if we are to be inspired by his method to fashion our own (complex, vitalist) methods—we have to start with and within our own experience.

Why does this claim matter for sustaining postpedagogy? We can begin with postpedagogy's insistence on singularity. Writing/teaching of any sort is so complex that no process or system can predict outcomes. Classroom ecologies will be too particular for replication; the best we can do is fashion a method of making ourselves susceptible to that particularity. But the experience of such particularities cultivates a certain continuity of experience. (Even to say that I cannot learn from the past is to admit having learned from the past.) My argument is that postpedagogy has not yet developed a philosophy of experience, a way of understanding how a previous Act might cultivate (or retard) a future Act, or how a previous ecology might cultivate (or retard) a future ecology. Perhaps that is because systemic approaches to pedagogy have been so dominant that disrupting them seems project enough. But we cannot finally disrupt human experience. The experience of learning can be generative or arresting, but it cannot be escaped. Therefore, experience is the only place (or time, or event) in which and through which we can discern a sustainable postpedagogical method—that is, a method that learns from previous situations while checking its own tendency to turn situations into systems. It is this argument to which I turn in the next chapter.

3

The Cultivation of Naïveté

> Nothing has brought pedagogical theory into greater disrepute
> than the belief that it is identified with handing out to teachers
> recipes and models to be followed in teaching.
>
> —John Dewey, *Democracy and Education*

TEACHING AS *TECHNE*

THE PHRASE "TEACHABLE MOMENT" WILL be familiar to teachers—those moments when, for reasons beyond your control or
planning, you realize that you can convey some particular lesson.
The postpedagogical school insists that this classroom *kairos* cannot be predicted or produced. We might rather call these moments
"teachable accidents." After all, how could any pedagogy reliably
occasion anything in a terrain made uncertain by a cacophony of
wills, desires, habits, and worries? Teaching, it seems, is more like
magic than science, more like alchemy than chemistry. These observations are not meant to cause despair. Clearly, teaching and
learning do happen in writing classrooms. It is just that the "pedagogical fantasy of control" (*Acts* 195), as Rickert calls it, cannot
guarantee teaching or learning. In fact, the best way to snuff out
such moments of discovery would be an attempt to produce them.

But what are we to do with them once they actually happen?
How do we incorporate such Acts, leaks, and emergences into our
continuing pedagogical work? Postpedagogical thought has dis-
equipped itself from asking this question. In its will to avoid system, postpedagogy has emphasized the disruptive. If there were a
motto for postpedagogy, we might find it in this sentence from
Nietzsche: "I mistrust all systematizers and I avoid them. The will
to a system is a lack of integrity" (470). I wonder, though, whether

such an emphasis can really move us toward new classroom ecologies. Ecologies are systems, after all. In an ecology, disruptions may be no more salutary than master plans; it all depends on the nature of the ecology.

Later in this chapter, I turn to John Dewey's notion of experience as a means of articulating a sustainable position for classroom ecologies. Before beginning that argument, however, I want to make a small detour through the teachable and the accidental, or at least their more ancient forebears: *techne* and *tuche*. The question that has occasioned this entire project—implicit until now—is whether, and how, we can see pedagogy as a *techne*. Can we, following Aristotle, "observe the cause why some succeed by habit and others accidentally," and can we agree that "such observation is the activity of an art [*techne*]" (*On Rhetoric* I.1.ii)? Let us stipulate Martha Nussbaum's definition of *techne* as "a deliberative application of human intelligence to some part of the world, yielding some control over *tuche*; [*techne*] is concerned with the management of need and with prediction and control concerning future contingencies" (95). Opposed to this deliberative application of human intelligence is *tuche*, or "what happens to a person by luck" or "what does not happen through his or her own agency, what just happens to him, as opposed to what he does or makes" (3). *Tuche* is what happens when you are making other plans. A carpenter may build a house well enough to withstand a storm but not the earthquake that collapses it. Likewise, a rhetorician may build an argument to persuade a hostile audience, only to discover—for reasons she could not anticipate—a much friendlier audience for whom the original arguments seem condescending or aggressive.

Nussbaum suggests that the tension between *techne* and *tuche* is one of the main springs of Greek philosophy, which turned to *techne* in search of a life less susceptible to contingency and uncertainty. But Greek drama, she writes, often questions the desire to rely too heavily on *techne*: "On the other side of this pursuit of self-sufficiency, complicating and constraining the effort to banish contingency from human life, was always a vivid sense of the special beauty of the contingent and the mutable, that love for the riskiness and openness of empirical humanity which finds its expression in recurrent stories about gods who fall in love with mortals" (3). Nussbaum does not simply claim that *tuche* cannot be avoided; in fact, she claims that it is a path (a road whose making cannot be predicted) to a special kind of beauty: "In our anxiety to control and grasp the uncontrolled by *techne*, we may all too easily become distant from the lives that we originally wished to control" (260). If the risk of *tuche* is that it opens the door to contingency, the risk of *techne* is that it closes the door to possibility. Taken too far, *techne* becomes hubris. The idea that *techne* would avoid the contingency of *tuche* altogether is "both futile and destructive: futile, because such a vantage point is unavailable, as such, to human inquiry; destructive, because the glory of the promised goal makes the humanly possible work look boring and cheap" (258). The fantasy of control is destructive and futile as a mere fantasy; it would be all the more destructive and futile if we could ever make it fact.

In asking whether pedagogy can be seen as a *techne*, I am introducing one of the most vexed terms in contemporary rhetoric and composition, where postmodern thought has undermined the idea that an art can be relied upon to produce certain outcomes. In her recent *Techne, from Neoclassicism to Postmodernism*, Kelly Pender captures the basic problem of *techne* by comparing the thought of Vitanza and Young, the former representative of a postmodern approach and the latter of a heuristic approach:

> If, taking a cue from Vitanza, we define a postmodern approach to writing as one that requires us to attend to the writing of accidents and the accidents of writing, and, taking a cue from Young, we define *techne* as the knowledge necessary for producing preconceived results by conscious, directed action, then it would appear that these two things—postmodernism and *techne*—are exact opposites. (87)

While Pender ultimately rejects this distinction, there is little doubt that the postpedagogical school emphasizes the possibilities of *tuche*. Sarah Arroyo, for example, argues that postpedagogy values "the aspect of chance. By giving up knowing in advance what outcomes will be, we open up a gigantic space for the potentiality of writing" (695). This potential space is also endorsed by Rickert's novelist, who insists that "every novel required new approaches and solutions to fresh problems that past writing experience could not cover" ("Toward" 263). Writ over the problems of pedagogy, the distinction between *techne* and *tuche* suggests two insupportable positions: either that teaching is a *techne* that ignores what it cannot predict or that learning is a product of *tuche*, invulnerable to the intervention of method or experience. Either way, teaching appears to remain impossible.

Yet, as Pender recounts, these may not be our only options. For the last twenty years, rhetoric and composition has been trying to fashion an understanding of *techne* that does not make it the enemy of *tuche*. In 1992, for example, Barbara Biesecker urged rhetorical scholars to "settle upon the word *techne* as the sign for an exorbitant doing that depends upon practice but which does not obey the imperatives of practice" ("Coming" 155). In this suggestion, we can see the basic vectors of the question of *techne*: surely there must be ways to develop *technai* that address contingency without extinguishing it, *technai* that allow us some agency within a situation without the damaging desire to be in complete control. Biesecker further suggests that we work "within and against the grain of the word's historically constituted semantic field" so that "*techne* can be used to refer to a kind of 'getting through' or ad hoc 'making do' by a subject whose resources are necessarily located in and circumscribed by the field within which she operates" (155). In this view, *techne* does not and cannot offer any prior guarantee of any product. Instead, *techne* operates "between intention and subjection, choice and necessity, activity and passivity" (156).[1] Six years later, Janet Atwill offered more historical ground for this idea of *techne* in *Rhetoric Reclaimed: Aristotle and the Liberal Arts Tradition*. Combing through Greek philosophy, myth, and literature, Atwill reconstructs a *techne* that challenges conventional concepts of virtue and subjectivity. Her research—like Nussbaum's—suggests that *techne* does not need to be reduced to purely instrumental understandings but that it has always been performed within (and *with*) contingency.

Unlike traditional humanism, Atwill argues, *techne* "is never a static, normative body of knowledge," it "resists identification with a normative subject," and it "marks a domain of human intervention and invention" (7). Most important for a project on sustainable pedagogy, Atwill also writes that *techne* is both "a set of transferable strategies" and "contingent on situation and purpose" (7). This claim revises the usual pedagogical conversation that pits the transferable against the contingent; instead, the relationship between the two is interdependent. Seasoned with ideas such as *kairos* and *metis* (the Greek term for craftiness or cunning) Atwill's *techne* needs contingency: the *techne* of the navigator needs the sea on which to sail (95). Recalling the discussion of Quintilian and Haynes in the first chapter, one might say that offshore is the only location in which *technai*—whether of writing or teaching—can take place.[2]

Pender adds her voice, urging rhetoric and composition to avoid its either-or tendency in "work that promotes *techne* to define it almost exclusively in positive terms (e.g., as a means of solving problems or inventing new social possibilities) and a corresponding tendency within work that critiques *techne* to define it almost exclusively in negative terms (e.g., a set of inflexible rules or a means of producing resources)" (*Techne* 38). Following Young, Pender describes a negative capability in which we see rational control not as an impediment to creation but rather as a catalyst for creation: "The art of rhetoric," she writes, "allows writers . . . to subject themselves—their plans, intentions, and goals—to the capriciousness and instability of their materials" (137). It is navigation that allows the sailor to get closest to the capriciousness and instability of the sea; it is rhetoric that allows the writer to get closest to the possibility and unpredictability of writing.

This exploration of *techne* challenges both commonplaces and anti-commonplaces about pedagogy. The will-to-system is to be avoided but so too is the will-to-anarchy. Hawk is right to point out that "technique consciously transferred through teaching cannot be simply applied to all occasions as an object controlled by a subject" ("Toward" 374). A *techne* is viable only insofar as it is receptive, and even susceptible, to the situation in which it unfolds. Hawk in fact endorses Cynthia Haynes's version of *techne* over Atwill's for precisely that reason: Haynes, he argues, emphasizes the subject's openness to the situation rather than the subject's intervention into the situation (382–83). He makes this judgment using three specific criteria, none of which is germane to the present argument; what is germane is that the notion of criteria suggests they must be prior to the situation in which they might be enacted. Otherwise, they would not be criteria. Hawk's posthumanist rhetor, therefore, brings something to a new situation that she has picked up in previous situations. This restores some degree of portability, even if it is a "paradoxical" portability. "Over time, and through practice, the student-rhetor who enacts these techniques in a specific workplace will get a sense of how to develop techniques that operate in these specific kinds of situations and would better anticipate the conditions of possibility of that enaction" (383–84). The same is true for Rickert's novelist, who, despite his claims, has learned (a) that he can write novels and (b) that he will have to relearn the techniques for writing them every time. These two important pieces of information teach him (and us) that we learn from experience. A truism, perhaps, but one that opens up a space for thinking about teaching after pedagogy.

The question is how we might turn that truism into a more rigorous and complex practice. The philosopher most ready to answer is Dewey, who made experience the centerpiece of his philosophic, or postphilosophical, project. It is in experience, "a concept that Dewey invokes in *every other area of his philosophy*" (Hildebrand 9), that I locate the possibility of a sustainable postpedagogy.[3] If pedagogy is a *techne*, experience is simultaneously its occasion and its material. Skills, strategies, and techniques may not be easily portable, but experience—both the teacher's and the learner's—cannot help but be portable, for it carries us as much as we carry it. In *Art as Experience* (1934), Dewey writes, "An instantaneous experience is an impossibility, biologically and psychologically. An experience is a product, one might almost say a by-product, of continuous and cumulative interaction of an organic self with the world" (229). If this is true, then the question for any pedagogy (including a pedagogy that resists its own systematizing tendencies in search of the "instantaneous") is how we can cultivate previous experience in a way that leads to more fruitful future experience. "It is not enough that certain materials and methods have proved effective with other individuals at other times. There must be a reason for thinking that they will function in generating an experience that has educative quality with particular individuals at a particular time" (*EE* 46).[4] In this statement, Dewey reveals himself to be a proto-postpedagogue, attuned both to the particulars of the moment and the way the past shapes those particulars. Dewey's educational project is to discern how we might cultivate the past and the present through method and by habit without reducing teaching to mere recipe writing. Therefore, I turn to Dewey for resources for sustaining postpedagogy.

My purpose here is to offer a theoretical framework for the deliberative pedagogical practice I articulate in the next chapter. Dewey himself might bristle at the idea of getting one's theoretical house in order before plunging into practice, for this all-too-common arrangement suggests the very separation between thought and work that Dewey rejects. Nevertheless, my ultimate aim of putting Dewey to work requires a focused discussion of his thought. To this end, what follows first is a traditional literature review, followed by my own engagement with Dewey. If nothing else, I hope to demonstrate that Dewey's work is particularly important now, at a moment when the field is no longer certain of its pedagogical methods or even of what role, if any, method should play in pedagogy.

TOWARD AN EXPLICIT TRADITION

As the author of some forty books, John Dewey presents a serious challenge to anyone who would risk the adjective *Deweyan* in any context. The scope of his interests—psychology, philosophy, education, political science, art, logic, ethics, intellectual history—makes him a daunting thinker to assess. Dewey lived ninety-two years, and his professional career lasted seventy. Grappling with his work therefore requires scholars to travel over a broad range. In addition, Dewey's work is not always easily accessible. Richard Hofstadter puts it bluntly in *Anti-Intellectualism in American Life*: "Dewey was hard to read and interpret" (361). This opacity has often under-mined understanding, as evidenced by the simple fact that Dew-ey had to defend himself from the charge of being a "Deweyan." Though he is associated with progressive education (most often, perhaps, by the enemies of progressive education), Dewey rejected the label, along with the practices that spawned it. His late *Experience and Education* (1938) represents an attempt to wrestle his own mantle back from his "progressive" disciples.

Given his interest in and attitudes toward education, it is not surprising that Dewey would be claimed for composition's "tacit tradition," as Janet Emig did in an article by that name. Seeking to shape the discipline of composition by sketching its intellectual heritage, Emig lists Polanyi (whose notion of the "tacit" provides the premise for Emig's argument), Vygotsky, Langer, Piaget, and many others as influences, but Dewey merits special mention: "John Dewey is everywhere in our work" (150).[5] Though Dewey did not often write about writing itself, when he does so, it is in language that prefigures our discipline's deepest wisdom:

> Children who begin with something to say and with intel-lectual eagerness to say it are sometimes made so conscious of minor errors in substance and form that the energy that should go into constructive thinking is diverted into anxiety not to make mistakes, and even, in extreme cases, into pas-sive quiescence as the best method of minimizing error. This tendency is especially marked in connection with the writing of compositions, essays, and themes. It has even been gravely recommended that little children should always write on triv-ial subjects and in short sentences because in that way they are less likely to make mistakes, while the teaching of writing to high school and college students occasionally reduces itself to a technique for detecting and designating mistakes. The resulting self-consciousness and constraint are only a part of the evil that comes from a negative ideal. (*HWT* 186–87)

Dewey wrote this in 1910, more than half a century before current-traditionalism came under serious critique. This passage would seem to lend support to Thomas Newkirk's claim in *More Than*

Stories: The Range of Children's Writing that "Dewey provides the soundest philosophical position for understanding and defending the writing-process approach" (200). In 1989, Newkirk deployed Dewey—quite correctly, in my view—in the fight against the "back-to-basics" movement, specifically E. D. Hirsch's *Cultural Literacy*, which had been published two years prior. As Newkirk insists, literacy, from the Deweyan point of view, is not merely a matter of names and dates. It is a matter, rather, of *transmission,* as Dewey understood the term, which refers more to cultural initiation than to content transfer (*DE* 4). Newkirk writes, "We transmit our culture to children not by handing something over to them, but by inviting and enabling their participation in communal action" (201). This notion of communal action is thoroughly Deweyan, for whom democratic culture was the highest desire. Yet Newkirk's reading of Dewey is nuanced; he understands that "it is necessary to disentangle the real Dewey from the popularized versions of Dewey, the shorthand that equates Dewey with Rousseau and with a value-neutral curriculum built exclusively on the interests of the child" (200). Should we continue to claim Dewey for composition, we will have to continue disentangling the real from the popularized.

The two most thorough engagements with Dewey were offered in the same year, 1998: Hephzibah Roskelly and Kate Ronald's *Reason to Believe* and Stephen M. Fishman and Lucille McCarthy's *John Dewey and the Challenge of Classroom Practice.* As we saw in the first chapter, Roskelly and Ronald argue that Dewey's philosophy reconciles practitioner and theorist, but they also find in Dewey's pragmatism grounds for other reconciliations. Like Newkirk, they complain that the real Dewey is still obscured by the popularized Dewey: "Dewey's legacy continues to be misread as merely romantic, not pragmatic or rhetorical" (97). As a result of this misreading, we also misread how Dewey's philosophy might ameliorate the temptation to succumb to either-or thinking—a propensity Dewey notes in *Experience and Education* (17). We seem to be left with two, and only two, choices: either a kind of ephemeral and intellectually thin "progressivism" or a rigid Taylor-esque efficiency, either the personal (dismissed by one side as "romantic") or the academic (dismissed by the other as "instrumental"). But pragmatism avoids these alternatives: "Pragmatism illuminates the rhetorical character of romanticism by explaining . . . mediation between individual limitation and individual possibility" (89). The question is not whether one needs to choose one over the other; one *cannot* choose one over the other, since the self is manifest in the social and the social in the self. Roskelly and Ronald thus urge composition to let go of its own false distinctions between expressivism and social constructivism, process and product, liberation and conformity. The promise of Dewey for composition, then, is that his work might help it resolve the dualisms that trouble our discipline.

The other 1998 book, Fishman and McCarthy's *John Dewey and the Challenge of Classroom Practice* (along with their earlier *College Composition and Communication* articles [Fishman; Fishman and McCarthy, "Teaching"]), offers the most sustained study of a Deweyan approach to classroom writing instruction. True to a Deweyan spirit, the authors do not simply write about Dewey; they work with him, putting his thought into practice. The book is a compelling combination of both intellectual autobiography and classroom inquiry, and it is the former struggle that inspired the latter project. Fishman, a philosophy professor and a scholar of Dewey, recounts his own struggle to understand the philosophic tradition during his own undergraduate and graduate study. Though Fishman studied at Columbia University (where Dewey spent most of his career and where many of Fishman's professors had studied and worked with Dewey himself), he encounters a curriculum that is nearly Dewey-free. By the time Fishman begins his education, analytic philosophy is ascendant, and Dewey—whose influence has never been as far-reaching as many of his critics have claimed—is nearly forgotten. Fishman pursues Dewey on his own, as a guide and even as a solace during his difficulties in becoming a professional philosopher: "I was puzzled about what happened to me between freshman and later university years, about my inability to be wholehearted about my schooling, to find continuities between myself and my professors, my courses and my life" (70). For Fishman, "whole heartedness" is perhaps the key educational value he takes from Dewey's *Democracy and Education* (173).

Having become a professor, Fishman strives to inspire whole-heartedness in his students—a way for them to connect the content of his course to their everyday experience. Frustrated, Fishman finds himself at a loss as to how he might reconstruct his own teaching. When he attends a writing-across-the-curriculum workshop, and then the Conference on College Composition and Communication convention, he concludes that the best way to revitalize his philosophic instruction is to revitalize his writing instruction. His philosophy courses thus become writing intensive. His partner in this effort is Lucille McCarthy, a compositionist who performs an ethnographic study of Fishman's attempts to link Deweyan content to an actual Deweyan approach. As McCarthy reports, Fishman at first experiences the same sort of difficulty described by Ann Berthoff in "Rhetoric as Hermeneutic": "We go from sentence combining to freewriting and back again to the formal outline; from vague notions of 'pre-writing' to vaguer notions of heuristics; from rigid rubrics to the idea of no writing at all" (279). McCarthy describes Fishman's difficulties in this way:

> At the end of every semester, he would ask his students to write an essay in which they connected a personal moral dilemma to some of the issues and texts they had talked about all term. And every semester he was disappointed. Students seldom succeeded in connecting their lives to Fishman's discipline. But when he tried to fix things, he only made matters worse. As if on a pedagogical pendulum, his adjustments to correct overemphasis on one member of the student-curriculum dualism resulted in overdevelopment of the other. (*John Dewey* 133)

The second half of the book follows the work of several of Fishman's philosophy students as they try to understand Dewey in their own terms—that is, to do philosophy as Dewey would have wanted. Like some of the most canonical work in composition, McCarthy's study continually forwards the actual writing of actual students. Through participant interviews, taped classroom sessions, and the students' own writing, McCarthy reveals a rich ecology of Deweyan inquiry and practice. Some students do manage to connect their own lives to the philosophy they are studying in Fishman's class. As compelling as this study is, however, it also implicitly raises an uncomfortable question for any compositionist who would teach in a Deweyan manner. Fishman's course, after all, is not a writing course; it is a content course with a writing emphasis. In this instance, writing serves another purpose rather than itself. Sánchez, for example, might quarrel with the fact that, once again, writing pursues the elusive "something else": "We firmly believe, despite our postmodern claims, in the presence of *something else* beyond the veil of language, and we have described it as being fundamentally apart from our language use, and we believe it to be theory's task to define and explain this noumenal realm" (10).

But this writing-vs.-content problem is also troubling from a Deweyan perspective, as David Russell suggests in "Vygotsky, Dewey, and Externalism: Beyond the Student/Discipline Dichotomy." Russell argues that Dewey's thought offers support for the "new abolitionist" movement. Composition, being extra-disciplinary, puts too much emphasis on the student instead of the (academic) subject. Russell rightly observes that Dewey did not endorse a "student-centered" curriculum at the expense of a "content-centered" curriculum. Among the dualisms that Dewey rejected is the "supposed opposition between the student and what is variously called content, subject matter, or academic discipline" (Russell, "Vygotsky" 174). Dewey also insisted that the student developed through interaction with traditional curricular subjects. In both *The Child and the Curriculum* (1902) and *Experience and Education* (1938), Dewey denies the idea that education should be primarily a matter of how and not a matter of what. Traditional school subjects provide the sort of texture required for a student to have a learning experience as Dewey means it. Dewey therefore scorned the idea that "progressive" education should ignore subject matter (Russell, "Vygotsky" 187). From this, Russell concludes that traditional first-year composition courses cannot help much in teaching students to write: "Unless they are involved (directly or vicariously) in the problems, activities, the habits of those who found a need to use writing in those ways, the discourse is meaningless—except as a requirement of a powerful institution" (194). For Russell, being Deweyan means the end of the stand-alone writing course.[6]

Thomas Kent's engagement with Dewey seems to portend similar conclusions about composition as a discipline. In *Paralogic Rhetoric*, Kent cites Dewey as part of his genealogy of paralogy, a genealogy that includes Nietzsche, Heidegger, and Wittgenstein and that provides a launching pad for the argument that writing is simply too situated to be understood or described in an abstract way. Dewey's transactional view of language is crucial to this reading. Language neither represents nor mediates but "is a public and collaborative process of human interaction" (*Paralogic* 10). It is, in a more current term in composition, emergent.[7] For Dewey, language is language only when and as it is used. As a rhetorician might observe, language does things, and the best education in language is an education in doing things with language. Those things, however, cannot constitute a process on which to build a discipline. Taken together, Russell and Kent see Deweyan thought as the end of composition studies as we know it.[8]

Other thinkers would simply argue that composition has posited dichotomies where none exists. Donald C. Jones, who worries that composition has not yet begun to grapple with Dewey's thought ("Beyond" 82), suggests that Peter Elbow's alleged "expressivism" was in fact far more pragmatic than commonly supposed. Free-writing, for example, "can both exploit language's influences on an individual and expose those influences to scrutiny" ("John Dewey" 270). Elbow's believing and doubting games offer the student the opportunity to apply "known concepts to new experiences and . . . to doubt each one as well" (271). Jones's larger project is to argue that composition's theoretical conversation mistakenly relies on "taxonomic distinctions known through induction for a fixed reality of absolute divisions" (274). These divisions between various theories are founded on the dualistic thinking that both Dewey's and Elbow's small *p* pragmatism rejects.

Nathan Crick makes a similar argument in his 2003 "Composition as Experience: John Dewey on Creative Expression and the Origins of 'Mind.'" Like Jones, Crick argues that composition has assumed a false dualism between self and society, this one leading us into a pointless debate about the origins of writing rather than the effects of writing (257). To insist that language is best understood as a product of a unified self or a social community is to insist on a distinction that is impossible to draw in the first place. The debate between Bartholomae and Elbow—so canonical in the evolution of composition theory—relies on the same basic premise: that writing represents thought, rather than instantiating both thought and action. "The experiences of students are taken as a given, and the compositions those students produce are considered representative texts rather than constitutive practices" (259). This position mirrors that of Roskelly and Ronald and Fishman and McCarthy, all of whom insist that expressivism–social construction is yet another of the dualisms Dewey would reject. Meanwhile, composition's tendency toward interpretation undermines the pragmatic possibility of Deweyan thought. That tendency, writes Crick, is not to ask "what art inspires, but what art reveals" (256).[9] A field inspired by Dewey would concentrate on the former. As with inspired adhoccery, art does not simply indicate some principle that resolves ambiguity; rather, art occasions further reconstruction and rethinking. Recall Fish's articulation of Taylor's principle: "the invoking and recharacterizing of rules and principles will often be components in the improvisation" (*Trouble* 64). Dewey might revise this claim to say that in any art or situation worth the name, the invoking and recharacterizing of rules, principles, or habits will always be components in the improvisation, or experience.

As these various inquiries suggest, Dewey offers a range of philosophical resources for a discipline that has wrestled with various dualisms: content-vs.-form, self-vs.-society, culture-vs.-information, etc. Because Dewey's entire project might be plausibly described as an overcoming of Hegel, it is little wonder that compositionists would turn to Dewey in an attempt to get past our particular dialectical conundrums. The question, then, is what we now need from Dewey, or which dualism we now need to surpass. This is a particularly critical question for postpedagogy, which might also be described as an overcoming of dualism and dialectic and which still wrestles with other troubling dualisms: order-vs.-surprise, control-vs.-freedom, pedagogy-vs.-something-that-comes-after-pedagogy. The anti-dualistic nature of the postpedagogical project can be seen in its reference to illegitimate couplings, ruptures, excesses, leaks, acts, occasion design rather than heuristics, jurisprudence rather than the law—anything that might offer a debauch against modernism's fastidious arrangements.

Dewey may seem a rather sober philosopher to turn to at this moment. So composed was Dewey that his older colleagues often assumed that there was not much "there" there (Menand 288). He also may seem a strange inspiration for a field concerned with writing. Even a brief perusal of his work will reveal that Dewey, while an exemplary public intellectual, was not always an exemplary stylist. Hofstadter dismisses his style as one of "terrible vagueness and plasticity" (361), and William James famously described Dewey's prose as "damnable; you might even say God-damnable" (qtd. in Hofstadter 361). Yet Dewey's style was a choice: Louis Menand reports that in his later writings, Dewey "deliberately adopted an antirhetorical style, in the belief that readers should be persuaded by the cogency of the thought rather than the felicities of the prose" (304). As Menand wryly observes, Dewey was "uncommonly successful at getting rid of the felicities" (304). Dewey himself admitted that writing was easier when he wrote his earliest articles, a time when his thinking depended on system rather than experience: "I imagine that my development has been controlled largely by a struggle between a native inclination toward the schematic and formally logical, and those incidents of personal experience that compelled me to take account of actual material" ("From Absolutism" 150). As that inclination gave way to Dewey's interest in everyday experience, writing became more demanding. In *Experience and Nature* (1925), he describes the challenge of writing in a new key: "A large part of the difficulty . . . is due to vocabulary. Our language is so permeated with consequences of theories which have divided the body and the mind from each other, making separate existential realms out of them, that we lack words to designate the actual existential fact" (284). The dualisms against which Dewey rebels (organism-vs.-environment, body-vs.-mind, word-vs.-deed, actor-vs.-scene) are such a familiar part of our mental furniture that it can be hard to rearrange writing.

Dewey's prose does provide moments of arresting insight. Whatever our opinion of his style, though, we should understand that Dewey considered communication fundamental to his philosophy. Society itself, he writes, "continues to exist by transmission, by communication, but it may fairly be said to exist in transmission, in communication" (*DE* 4). In Burkean terms, communication is both agent and scene. Dewey also describes language as "a great, perhaps the greatest of all, educational resources [sic]" (*SS* 43) and the "tool of tools" (*EN* 168). *Tool* should not suggest a merely instrumental attitude toward education; to be the ultimate tool is to be the occasion and the grounding of all other tools. When Dewey calls language the "tool of tools," he is placing it at the center of his philosophy, just as contemporary compositionists might. Dewey's attitude toward language insists on its centrality but avoids reducing experience to a mere linguistic construct. This is the crucial contribution Dewey offers to a field that no longer has confidence in foundations. As Donald Jones observes, "If one attends to the premises of Dewey's mature thought, they lead to profound philosophical and social transformations. The non-foundational alternative of Deweyan pragmatism heralds anti-foundationalism's subsequent emphasis on language without ignoring the epistemological importance of experience" ("Beyond" 88). In Dewey's mind, one does not have to choose between threatening reality with the primacy of language or deflating language with the weight of reality. Like any tool, language wields its power to shape even while it also must yield to that which is being shaped.

Dewey's struggle against dualism should attract continuing interest from the "teaching discipline," which has long fretted over the supposed distinction between theory and practice. A deeper engagement with Dewey will further a project first outlined by Louise Wetherbee Phelps in *Composition as a Human Science*. Phelps turns to Dewey to bolster her case that composition must be able to articulate a praxis that unites rather than divides theory and practice.

Dewey, Phelps observes, sees experience as "the testing ground (praxis) where reflective concepts can be experimentally verified" (210). Dewey's critique of traditional philosophy is that it never returns to the testing ground, and his empiricism asks that it do so. To put it more precisely, theory that remains untested by experience is not really theory. Dewey's use of the term *experience* is in fact meant to obviate this binary. In his view, experience includes both the raw data of everyday living as well as the reflection on the experience that shapes our understanding of the future and (re) shapes our understanding of the past. My argument is that this notion of experience can help composition articulate and sustain teaching in a postpedagogical field. Making this argument requires a careful explication of Dewey's thought, an explication that I offer in the next section.

THE METHOD AND THE REWARD

Like every other keyword in the Deweyan lexicon, *experience* carries multiple meanings. Rather than being dualistic, experience is "double-barrelled" (a formulation that Dewey borrows from William James). It "includes *what* men do and suffer, *what* they strive for, love, believe and endure, and also *how* men act and are acted upon, the ways in which they do and suffer, desire and enjoy, see, believe, imagine—in short, processes of *experiencing*" (*EN* 8). Dewey accuses traditional philosophy—by which he tends to mean Platonic and Enlightenment philosophy—of avoiding the change and contingency of everyday living. "Gross experience," he writes, "is loaded with the tangled and complex; hence philosophy hurries away from it to search out something so simple that the mind can rest trustfully in it, knowing that it has no surprises in store, that it will not spring anything to make trouble, that it will stay put, having no potentialities in reserve" (*EN* 26). Dewey's early idealism had once led him to search for absolute foundations, but his interest in social improvement eventually convinced him that philosophy had to be involved in the ongoing change that characterizes life. True philosophy, argues Dewey, begins with "the traits which are characteristic of thinking, namely, uncertainty, ambiguity, alternatives, inquiring, search, selection, experimental reshaping of external conditions" (*EN* 69). It locates itself in becoming rather than being, in drama rather than exposition.

One might turn to many places in Dewey's work for a definition of *experience*, but a compelling version can be found in his 1934 *Art as Experience*: "Experience is the result, the sign, and the reward of that interaction of organism and environment which, when it is carried to the full, is a transformation of interaction into participation and communication" (22). This tripartite definition—result, sign, reward—captures the complexity of what Dewey is pursuing in experience. It is the result, or data, of interaction; the sign, or evidence, of that interaction; and the reward, or the meaning, of that interaction. As we will see when we turn to Dewey's thoughts on education, experience—like the environment in which and through which it occurs—is something that can be ignored or cultivated, but it cannot finally be avoided. While ideas like organism and environment can be separated analytically, they cannot finally be separated in actual experience. "Borrower cannot borrow without lender to lend[,] . . . the loan being a transaction that is identifiable only in the wider transaction of the full legal-commercial system" (*KK* 133). Human behavior is ecological: "Mind, body, and world are mutually created by their ongoing interaction" (Hildebrand 21). Just as Dewey anticipates the idea of writing as ecology, he anticipates posthumanism: "Organisms . . . live, that is, as much in processes across and 'through' skins as in processes 'within' skins. One might as well study an organism in complete detachment from its environment as try to study an electric clock on the wall in disregard of the wire leading to it" (*KK* 128). To say that one is an organism is to say at the same time that one is environmental—that is, the result, the sign, and the reward of operating within an environment.

Dewey suggests that opening oneself to life (to *tuche*, to *kairos*) is philosophically counterintuitive. The quest for certainty has led philosophy in search for meaning "invulnerable to vicissitude," a desire that has "disjoined" thought "from all that is empirical" (*EN* 167). For Dewey, however, the empirical represents the world of change and the world of possibility—that is, the world of experience. Dewey's understanding of the word *empirical* can be captured by recalling its etymology: in Greek, *empeiria* means "experience." Dewey's basic project is to wed the empirical and the philosophical: "Empirically, things are poignant, tragic, beautiful, humorous, settled, disturbed, comfortable, annoying, barren, harsh, consoling, splendid, fearful; are such immediately and in their own right and behalf" (96). It is within that sort of experiential variety that Dewey locates philosophy. His point is not merely to put abstract ideas to a practical test; rather, it is that ideas have power only within the practical world of everyday living. This is what it means to "intellectualize practice" (Eldridge 5). Dewey's philosophy is unabashedly empiricist, but it is an empiricism that operates within the complexity of everyday experience.

Among language-speaking beings, the activity between an organism and an environment is manifest through communication, whose duties are both to get things done and to maintain sociable relations. "The primary motive for language," Dewey writes in *How We Think* (1910), "is to influence (through the expression of desire, emotion, and thought) the activity of others; its secondary use is to enter into more intimate sociable relations with them; its employment as a conscious vehicle of thought and knowledge is a tertiary, and relatively late, formation" (179). Dewey insists that philosophy has gone wrong by embracing this third task at the expense of the other two.

That does not mean, however, that Dewey fails to recognize language as a conscious vehicle of thought and knowledge. Communication is neither solely a means nor an end, neither solely instrumental nor solely consummatory: "Discourse itself is both instrumental and consummatory. Communication is an exchange which procures something wanted. . . . Communication is also an immediate enhancement of life, enjoyed for its own sake" (*EN* 183). At times, the instrumental seems to come first for Dewey insofar as he sees it as the most common motive for communication. But in Dewey's rhetorical universe, it is "communication, language, discourse" that cross the "factitious and gratuitous" gulf between "existence and essence" (167). Language is a way of doing everyday work and making everyday meaning, but it is also a way of reorienting the basic philosophic assumptions that Dewey wants to contest. He therefore calls communication a "wonder by the side of which transubstantiation pales" (166). It is in this wonder that communication transforms experience from raw data to shared meaning. Indeed, one of the central dualisms that Dewey rejects is that between communication and experience. In the terms of contemporary composition, he does not believe the idea that language is merely representational, the assumption to which Sánchez also objects (10). Dewey says that "to be a recipient of a communication is to have an enlarged and changed experience" (DE 5). Communication is both the way in which and the experience through which we overcome dualisms that limit understanding. It accomplishes and evokes and therefore becomes intelligence: "When the instrumental and final functions of communication live together in experience, there exists an intelligence which is the method and reward of the common life, and a society worthy to command affection, admiration, and loyalty" (EN 205). Intelligence is simultaneously means and end, an activity rather than a thing, a practice rather than a quality.

Not surprisingly, Dewey's view of language lends a rhetorical cast to his education philosophy.[10] In "My Pedagogic Creed" (1897), Dewey writes, "It is true that language is a logical instrument, but it is fundamentally and primarily a social instrument. Language is the device for communication; it is the tool through which one individual comes to share the ideas and feelings of others" (434). This fundamental social feature and nature makes language "perhaps the greatest of all . . . educational resources" (SS 43).[11] The purpose of education, therefore, should be to cultivate this already present resource as productively as possible. The urge to use language, Dewey reasons, is an urge not to represent but to communicate and to accomplish. Another dualism—this time between language and world, or rhetoric and reality—is thus rejected: "Taken literally, the maxim, 'Teach things, not words,' or 'Teach things before words,' would be the negation of education; it would reduce mental life to mere physical and sensible adjustments" (*HWT* 176). Mental life, however, is about making meaning as well as adjustments. Through language, "man is lifted from his immediate isolation and shares in a communion of meanings" (*EN* 205). Language occasions and enables the sharing of experience, which Dewey calls "the greatest of human goods" (202). The promise of experience is that it can be "instrumental as liberating us from the otherwise overwhelming pressure of events and enabling us to live in a world of things that have meaning. It is final as a sharing in the objects and arts precious to a community" (204–5). Crucially—particularly for a field that has sometimes been enamored of "liberatory" pedagogies—this is not a liberation *from* so much as a liberation *for*, for making meaning of the everyday experience that traditional philosophy has often dismissed as too contingent and changeable. Any experience—communicated to self and others through language— is available for meaning. "Even the dumb pang of an ache," he writes, "achieves a significant existence when it can be designated and descanted upon; . . . it has the dignity of an office" (167). The question becomes how we designate and descant, how, that is, we make an office out of everyday living.

Dewey's philosophical project is to discern methods by which primary experience—experience-as-data—can be transformed into secondary experience—experience-as-equipment-for-living. "Primary," for Dewey, refers to experience in an "uncontrolled form," "secondary" to "a more regulated and significant form—a form made possible by the methods and results of reflective experience" (*EN* 15). Each sort of experience forms and informs the other. Unless we use the reflective equipment we fashion, we cannot claim to have learned from primary experience, and secondary experience becomes nothing more than pure abstraction. The secondary, therefore, must always be retested within the primary: "The charge that is brought against the non-empirical method of philosophizing is not that it depends upon theorizing, but that it fails to use refined, secondary products as a path pointing and leading back to something in primary experience" (6). This basic idea also lies at the heart of Dewey's education theory. In *The Child and the*

Curriculum (1902), he describes his pedagogical method as one which "intervenes between the more casual, tentative, and round-about experiences of the past, and more controlled and orderly experiences of the future. It gives past experience in that net form which renders it most available and most significant, most fecund for future experience" (*SS* 199). We can see here the rhetorical cast of Dewey's thought: the past is not merely a motley of experiences but rather a vein that can be mined through method into resources for invention. The past must be converted into a resource; otherwise, theory and philosophy cannot claim to have what William James called "cash-value." Dewey's question is simple: "Does [a philosophy, a theory] end in conclusions which, when they are referred back to ordinary life-experiences and their predicaments, render them more significant, more luminous to us, and make our dealings with them more fruitful?" (*EN* 7). This question articulates what Dewey calls "a first-rate test" of any philosophy or theory: how does the practice of intentional reflection allow me to render my experience more meaningful and more useful? Intelligence is therefore "associated with *judgment*; that is, with selection and arrangement of means to effect consequences and with choice of what we take as our ends" (*QC* 170). One does not "have" intelligence; rather, one engages (in) intelligence.

To obtain the rewards of experience requires that we intervene in experience by means of a method. Practice is always already what we have been doing; experience is always already what we have been having. Method—the way we intervene in the unfolding events—is what makes it possible to intellectualize practice. "Organic interaction becomes inquiry when existential consequences are anticipated; when environing conditions are examined with reference to their potentialities; and when responsive activities are selected and ordered with reference to actualization of some of the potentialities, rather than others, in a final existential situation" (Dewey, *Logic* 107). Everyday living becomes method when we examine the world around us, when we make guesses as to the consequences our various choices might produce, and when we make choices and see whether they work. To be alive in a clinical sense is to be in organic interaction. To be alive in a Deweyan sense is to make a method of that organic interaction.

For Dewey, method, or empirical inquiry, should not be limited to scientific questions but should rather become the basis for meaningful living. But neither does empiricism mean that we simply apply practices of science to everyday living. As Dewey makes clear in the second and sixth chapters of his *Logic* (1938), the aims of scientific inquiry and what he calls "common sense" inquiry are different, but the basic method is the same and in many ways will seem familiar. Dewey's method of inquiry begins with a *situation*. This term carries obvious resonances for scholars in rhetoric and composition,[12] where the argument comes down to a couple of basic questions: Does a situation present itself, or do we present ourselves to it? Do we perceive a situation, or do we construct it? And can something called a "situation" ever be isolated—whether by perception or construction—from continuous experience? Does rhetoric really work only when we have cordoned off something we have called a situation so that we can then intervene in it? Dewey is acutely aware of these problems, and his nondualistic philosophy attempts to work around the binaries that occasion them. For example, an organism is what it is because it interacts with an environment. A butterfly pinned in a glass case, separated from its ecology, is no longer a butterfly in the richest sense of the term. This is just as true for the human being, who is a human being because she operates within some environment. "What is designated by the word 'situation' is *not* a single object or event or set of objects and events. For we never experience nor form judgments about objects and events in isolation, but only in connection with a contextual whole. The latter is what is called a 'situation'" (*Logic* 66). That contextual whole includes the habits, affect, and history brought by the experience.

From some of his earliest work in psychology, Dewey claimed that a situation could not simply be understood as stimulus-response, as though the subject were a blank screen waiting for a situation to be projected upon it. In "The Reflex Arc Concept in Psychology," for example, Dewey insists that stimulus-response can be separated only for analysis, not in the actual situation. "What we have is a circuit," he writes, "not an arc or broken segment of a circle. This circuit is more truly termed organic than reflex, because the motor response determines the stimulus, just as truly as sensory stimulus determines movement" (102). Our response shapes what we are responding to, just as what we are responding to shapes our response. There is no meaningful separation between the two. The phrase "what we are responding to" begs a question that has to be begged. How, then, do we designate a situation? Dewey would ask the question differently (and more rhetorically): what occasions a situation? The answer is deceptively simple: a problem. In a sense, the clichéd movie euphemism—"Mr. President, we have a situation on our hands"—is precisely what Dewey means. Inquiry begins when a problem arises, when something is out of joint. Method begins when some new experience upsets the way of proceeding we have constructed from previous experience. We have a situation on our hands when our habits no longer seem to serve. (The same is true for Dewey's ethical theory, as we see in Chapter 4.)

My argument is that postpedagogy is good at articulating the upset, so to speak, but not what follows it. The question of whether our upset is "mere" perception or "nothing more than" construction is beside the point. Of course we respond to some stimulus, and of course our response to that stimulus is shaped by our predisposition to it. What makes a situation a situation is that our familiar habits of response are challenged by the unforeseen and unanticipated. The method of inquiry is how we put our present problem in conversation with previous experience in order to shape future action. Pedagogy cannot and indeed should not anticipate situations so well that they are no longer situations. *Techne* cannot and should not foreclose *tuche*. But experience is a part of *techne*, and a pedagogy—even a situated rather than a systematized pedagogy—has to be able to articulate the role of experience.

For Dewey, education is the art of intentionally creating situations with an eye toward the student's growth. Education is in fact "occasion design." The Deweyan educator begins to create such situations by opening the curriculum to the desires and impulses of the students, much in the way that Hawk describes: "Students would need to, and be encouraged to, work out their own constellations that would mix our curriculum with their contexts, our theories and methods with their political interests—should they have them" (*Counter-History* 219). Dewey also insists that student desire and interest must motivate the encounter with the curriculum. But this encounter with the curriculum is essential, and the teacher takes an active role in directing that encounter into the most productive channels. This is a serious demand, so serious that it is hard to imagine how Dewey was ever interpreted to be suggesting a reduced role for the teacher. As he makes clear in *Experience and Education*, Dewey laments situations "in which children are . . . left entirely to themselves, the teacher being loath to suggest even what might be done with the materials lest freedom be infringed upon" (71). Because Dewey defines the human as a creature who lives with other humans, he rejects the simplistic idea of freedom adopted by some of his epigones. Hawk agrees that the freedom of the learner does not entail the absence of the teacher: "Rather than set the context or problem and then let students work out solutions on their own, a complex vitalist method makes the teacher a crucial part of the ecology" (*Counter-History* 254). Dewey might read this as a descriptive statement as much as an argumentative one. To be a human, in Dewey's estimation, is already to be within an ecology; to be a teacher is already to be within an educative ecology. Good pedagogy represents the acknowledgment of and the engagement with that ecology.

Yet Dewey's vision of the teacher's role is even more robust: "In an *educational* scheme, the occurrence of a desire and impulse is not the final end. It is an occasion and a demand for the formation of a plan and method of activity. . . . The teacher's business is to see that the occasion is taken advantage of" (*EE* 71). The word *scheme* may not be any more palatable than *system,* given the contours of the conversation thus far.[13] But it does point to Dewey's belief that the teacher plays a major role in the unfolding of education. Occasions will shape future experience one way or another; the only question for Dewey is whether and how we might help students cultivate those situations. "A well-trained mind," he writes, "is one that has a maximum of resources behind it, so to speak, and that is accustomed to go over its past experiences to see what they yield" (*DE* 157). Developing and sustaining those resources is the work of education, and it is here that we ourselves can find resources for developing and sustaining the postpedagogical project.

LEARNING THE USES OF EXPERIENCE

Like many in the postpedagogical school, Dewey sees the fundamental experiential situation as a disruption—that is, as an experience that interrupts the usual and the familiar. Learning happens when some event challenges our usual habits and practices. What separates Dewey from postpedagogy, however, is the central role of experience in his method. For Dewey, experience is the crux of learning. The experience of disruption itself is born, in part, of previous experience, and the way we assimilate disruption will shape future experience. For example: A student writer has always been able to get a good grade by sitting down and cranking out a single draft the night before an assignment is due. Then one day—in his first-year comp course, say—he follows this procedure and finds himself with an *F*. He now has some data that contradict his usual habit; the only question is how he will interpret this new experience through his previous experience and how he will act going forward. He might conclude that his teacher is unfair or that he hates English. Or he might conclude that his usual way of proceeding has to change. All of these count as reflections of one sort or another, and all will lead to some future action—either doing things differently than before or sticking to the plan. If this *F* is a one-off event, perhaps the student is right to maintain his habits; if it happens a few more times, he might be inclined to reconsider. Either way, Dewey's understanding of experience—and his attempt to turn experience into a method—begins with his insistence that a disruptive event is disruptive insofar as it occurs within an ecology of the student's own experience.

Thus far in this chapter, I have only hinted at the significance of ecology in Dewey's thought. Ecology has also become significant in composition. Starting with Marilyn Cooper's 1989 "The Ecology of Writing" and culminating most recently with Jenny Edbauer's 2005 "Unframing Models of Public Distribution," composition has moved steadily toward "ecology" as the master metaphor for how and where writing happens. Cooper explicitly offers ecology as a replacement for process, whose fate she captures with this terse observation: "Revolution dwindles to dogma" (2). Process, as Cooper argues in terms reminiscent of Dewey, is separated from the social. Then, in seemingly un-Deweyan fashion, Edbauer insists that process is too atomistic to account for complex rhetorical action. Both settle on ecology. Cooper describes "the ideal image" of the ecological model as "an infinitely extended group of people who interact through writing, who are connected by the various systems that constitute the activity of writing" (12). Edbauer adds that a "rhetorical situation is better conceptualized as a mixture of processes and encounters" (13). Both challenge rhetorical theorists to see the full complexity of rhetoric's topography, and, having "relocated" writers within this rich landscape, both also echo Deweyan tones. Cooper argues that writing "is not simply a way of thinking but more fundamentally a way of acting" (13), and Edbauer observes that pedagogy should not be "'*learning* by doing,' but '*thinking* by doing.' Or, better yet, "*thinking/doing*—with a razor thin slash mark barely keeping the two terms from bleeding into each other" (23).

In the end, though, Cooper and Edbauer confront composition's familiar difficulty: Edbauer offers rhetorical ecologies as "a rethinking of the 'in order to later' model, where students learn methods, skills, and research *in order to later* produce at other sites" (23). Here again, she echoes Dewey, ever-suspicious of learning that is not meaningful to the learner as she is learning. Locating the fruit of our labors at some unknown future date divorces the learner from learning. Cooper simply adds that "looking at writing ecologically we understand better how important writing is—and just how hard it is to teach" (13). We return to the problem of portability and of complexity. Is writing so complex as to be unportable? Perhaps, then, we should concentrate on the ecology before us. Yet the future is always lurking in the pedagogical imagination: even to reject the "in order to later" model of teaching is to acknowledge that learning is for the future as well as the present. It is impossible to argue for enriching the present without tacitly seeing that present as a resource for an as-yet-unknown future.

Experience is the vehicle by which we carry learning from the present into the future. When we speak of an ecology's "effects, enactments, and events" (Edbauer 9), we are speaking of experience—the experience of operating within an ecology. But we are not simply organisms that operate within ecologies. We ourselves are ecologies, and as in all ecologies, events of the past affect the present and linger into the future. Experience-as-method is Dewey's way of cultivating the ecology of the self. That cultivation, however, is not exclusively with the self. As we might expect, Dewey defines the self as a social being, and interactions with others have lasting effects on the shape of the self. In *Ethics*, he writes, "A person may realize that a certain act is trivial in its effects upon others and in the changes it impresses upon the world; and yet he may hesitate to perform it because he realizes it would intensify some tendency of his own in such a way as, in the delicate economy of character, to disturb the proper balance of the springs of action" (Dewey and Tufts 354). The delicate economy (or ecology) of character is shaped by what Dewey calls continuity. Our present experiences cannot help but be informed by our previous experiences. "Just as no man lives or dies to himself," Dewey writes, "so no experience lives and dies to itself. Wholly independent of desire or intent, every experience lives on in further experiences" (*EE* 27). New experiences do not simply overwrite old experiences. The new shapes the old and vice versa. Whatever happens in our present experience, that experience will have some effect on our perception of an action in future experience. Individuals, Dewey writes, "live in a series of situations. And when it is said that they live *in* these situations, the meaning of the word 'in' is different from its meaning when it is said that pennies are 'in' a pocket or paint is 'in' a can. It means, once more, that interaction is going on" (43). Again, conventional language habits hamper Dewey's expression. It might be more accurate to say that individuals live in and through situations or that they live with(in) them.

The central problem of education is how experience is to be cultivated. "The continuity of any experience, through renewing of the social group, is a literal fact. Education, in its broadest sense, is the means of this social continuity of life" (*DE* 2). Education, in other words, can be understood as the method of inquiry by which we make continuity into a resource for future experience. In Dewey's works on education, we can most clearly see how his experimental method is essentially an attempt to cultivate experience. In *The School and Society* (1900/1915), for example, he describes what he means by experience turned into a method: "It intervenes between the more casual, tentative, and roundabout experiences of the past, and more controlled and orderly experiences of the future. It gives past experience in that net form which renders it most available and most significant, most fecund for future experience" (199). In *Democracy and Education* (1916), Dewey defines education itself as a "reconstruction or reorganization of experience which adds to the meaning of experience and which increases ability to direct the course of subsequent experiences" (76). This definition suggests again the James-inspired, Deweyan double-barrelled notion of primary experience transformed through method into secondary experience. In "My Pedagogic Creed," Dewey writes, "education must be conceived as a continuing reconstruction of experience; that the process and the goal of education are one and the same thing" (434). Throughout these passages, we are reminded of the double meaning that Dewey attaches to this "double-barrelled" word: there is both experience-as-data and experience-as-method. Education is the process of turning the former into the latter. This work is not always pleasant or easy. "For 'taking in' in any vital experience is something more than placing something on the top of consciousness over what was previously known. It involves reconstruction which may be painful" (*AE* 42). Reconstruction, however, is not an interruption in continuity; it is an embrace of continuity in order to invent new resources for action.

At this point, *process* may be a dangerous word to use. Yet Dewey's process, or method, is effectively postpedagogical: it is not a precise algorithm, but rather the simple demand that the products of reflection and inquiry be tested in reencounters with the new experience. Our conclusions must "be confirmed or modified by the new order and clarity they introduce into [the experience out of which they arose], and the new significantly experienced objects for which they furnish a method" (*EN* 18). It is not enough merely to reflect on previous experiences; those reflections must find their way back into new practices. Only then does experience move from an event to a method. The work of pedagogy is simply to turn experience-as-data into experience-as-method. More important, the empirical cast of that method prevents it from becoming a process in the negative sense of the term. Because Dewey's method requires reencounter with experience-as-data, it cannot be turned into an algorithm: for the reflective subject, there will always be new experience to challenge previous habits. That does not mean, however, that we can never rely on previous habits to see us through a great deal of experience. For Dewey, a situation is a situation precisely because it challenges what we learn from our experience.

This idea of continuity is at once the challenge to postpedagogy and the opportunity for its own renewal and extension. Because the postpedagogical school is so concerned with the excess, the leak, and the Act, it does not look at how those events must be related to what has come before and what comes after. I mean "must be" here in both a prescriptive and descriptive sense. Present experience will be shaped by previous experience and will shape future experience; therefore, education ought to be in the business of intervening in this process to make it as productive as possible. If the self is an ecology, then education is the work of cultivating that ecology. Experience is not the mere aggregate of lessons learned, as though they are collected in a pile. It instead operates through continuity, the "continual readaptation of the environment to the needs of living organisms" (*DE* 2). Organisms live through constant readaptation or, we might say, constant revision. As in revision, we do not simply repeat what has come before, nor do we erase it.

Contrary to postprocess, then, rhetorical sensitivity does not require the repeated reinvention of the wheel, as Thomas Kent seems to suggest. For Kent, nearly any attempt to apply the lessons of previous experience to future situations is inevitably a distortion. No such predictions can be made, Kent reasons, since any new rhetorical situation will present new circumstances. In the words of Donald Davidson, on whom Kent most often relies, our "prior" theories—what we believe about utterances prior to a specific situation—cannot predict our "passing" theories—what we use for interpretation when we actually hear an utterance (*Paralogic* 86). Prior theories cannot accurately predict the work we may have to do in a rhetorical situation; therefore, we have to construct temporary passing theories for new situations. This is the basic argument that has undermined the process paradigm upon which so much of composition's early work was built. Kent momentarily turns to Dewey to bolster this argument for paralogy, which he defines as "the unpredictable, elusive, and tenuous decisions or strategies we employ when we actually put language to use" (*Paralogic* 3). He notes correctly the importance of communication to Dewey's thought and persuasively infers that Dewey believes language cannot be reduced to a "set of codifiable speech acts" (11). Yet he admits that that observation "does not deliver us all the way home" to paralogy (11). It is easy to see why: Dewey's empirical method does make communication an act of experimentation, but it is an experimentation from which we learn. By making a method of experience, Dewey seeks to cultivate the continuity that is already there.

Yet that continuity also complicates Kent's attempt to cast invention as nonrenewable. Kent insists that prior theories guarantee nothing, which is true enough. What he de-emphasizes is that passing theories will be made, at least in part, of prior theories. In the terms I articulated in Chapter 1, Kent's paralogy and postprocess are purely ad hoc. But the paradox of purity, as Burke reminds us, is that purity cancels itself out. "Pure Personality," Burke writes, "would be the same as No Personality" (*Grammar* 35). Pure invention is no invention. This is another way of making Pender's point about *techne* (*Techne*). It is invention—an art that we can carry with us from one situation to the next—that allows us to encounter uncertainty in the first place (137). Without a prior theory, a passing theory is impossible.

In order to rely on Dewey to make his paralogic argument, Kent has to ignore Dewey's writings on education, for it is there that Dewey describes continuity. Obviously, explicating Dewey is no easy task, but any explication that neglects Dewey's writings on education ignores the heart of his work. Dewey is not a philosopher who took a passing interest in education. In addition to being the founder of the Chicago Laboratory School, Dewey had once considered the possibility of giving up his pursuit of formal philosophy to "teach it via pedagogy" (Menand 319), and he saw education as "the one form of social life . . . which is directly experimental" (320).[14] To acknowledge the experimental in Dewey's philosophy would undermine Kent's claims about the singularity of new situations. It is hard to imagine that Dewey would deny the centrality of passing theories; the difference is that Dewey has more faith that our passing theories can teach us something about our present experience. While Kent acknowledges that new communication requires "a kind of impromptu hermeneutic dance choreographed by our prior and passing theories," the emphasis in the following claim is misplaced: "Once communication takes place . . . the passing theory, in a sense, disappears to become part of a prior theory that may or may not be used in future communicative situations" (*Paralogic* 87). For Dewey, such experiences do not disappear so much as become available means for the shaping of future practice. Kent would seem to downplay these effects, but they are precisely what Dewey wants to cultivate: "The 'new' is, in all cases, relatively, not absolutely, new. Even though something absolutely new may be desirable . . . , the continuities in culture and experience exclude the possibility of anything having in fact this absolute character" (Dewey, Introduction ix–x).[15] Continuity stretches between experiences.

True, "no framework theory of any kind can help a student predict in advance the interpretation that someone else may give to an utterance" (Kent, *Paralogic* 161), but "framework," which here is meant to bear all the philosophical weight, is not the only available means for learning from prior experience. As we saw with the House of Lore in Chapter 1, a framework that imposes a structure deductively (or even inductively) can be distinguished from one that grows a structure through cultivation. Experience is also something of an old manse, one that may be delightful, or haphazard, or troubling, depending on the ways in which new experience is added on to old experience. In North's old manse of lore, the accretion of experience seems to happen in an entirely random fashion. But that is not the way of experience, at least as Dewey understands it. Experiences do not simply pile up on top of one another. They are "inherently relational: we do not begin with atomized bits of experience and then subsequently stitch them together" (Hildebrand 44). As Burke might say, the casuistic stretch between the old and the new cannot be eliminated. Dewey's philosophy of education is based on the idea that the stretch can be practiced.

If it seems as though I am focusing excessively on Kent's idea of paralogy, it is because Kent has been one of the most powerful voices urging composition away from pedagogy hope and theory hope. He is also the earliest of the postprocess school to articulate its starkest claim: "Writing and reading—conceived broadly as processes or bodies of knowledge—cannot be taught, for nothing exists to teach" (*Paralogic* 161). This argument—if we take it seriously—forces us to reconsider the very nature of our discipline. Like Aristotle, we have sometimes hoped that we could observe the processes of the successful and then reproduce them in our classrooms. As North observes in *The Making of Knowledge in Composition*, it was this methodological move that occasioned the modern discipline, a move that simultaneously sought to "replace practice as the field's dominant mode of inquiry" (15). What makes Kent's postprocess radical is its attack on this methodological need. Indeed, given the Deweyan investments of my own argument, I should simply endorse Kent's argument, which seems to return us to practice. In fact, Kent professes a Deweyan notion of teachers as mentors or coworkers "who actively collaborate with their students to help them through different communication situations" and who become "an integral part of their students' learning experiences" (*Paralogic* 166). This view echoes what we have seen from Dewey, Hawk, and Berthoff.

Less persuasive, however, is Kent's notion of learning and invention, which denies the role experience plays in each. Even the idea of "mentorship" depends on the assumption that the mentor possesses something or transports something from one situation into another, a possibility that undermines Kent's entire argument. What is mentorship except a communication of experience? The distinction here is between method-as-process and method-as-experience. Kent's target is the former, and his claim is that situations are too unpredictable to be easily susceptible to method-as-process. This is true enough, though it depends on a reductive notion of process as "the inoculation concept of writing," which "holds we can become effective writers if only we receive a pedagogical injection of efficacious rules" ("Preface" xvii). Whatever capital P Process eventually became, its earlier proponents would likely not recognize themselves in Kent's description. Any claims to radicalness disappear the moment Kent speaks of gathering the "background knowledge" that he admits will make guesses more accurate (*Paralogic* 168). Kent's use of "guesswork" in this context is a bit slippery, and it fails to distinguish between shots in the dark and informed hypotheses. The difference between the two lies within the experience the mentor and the mentored bring to a situation.

Let us grant that writing cannot be taught as a process or a body of knowledge. The more urgent question is whether writing can be cultivated as experience. Kent's idea of mentorship suggests that it can be so cultivated. But that leaves all our work ahead of us. When Ann Berthoff reminds us that out of nothing, nothing can be made, and when she insists that we should be "Learning the Uses of Chaos," she is also reminding us of teaching's highest aspiration. This same aspiration motivates Dewey's pedagogical/philosophical process, which wants to live within uncertainty, ambiguity, alternatives, inquiry, search, selection, and—most important—the experimental reshaping of external conditions. That reshaping is the work of teaching. It is work closer to Kent's vision than it is to traditional visions, but it is teaching nonetheless. Kent envisions a classroom in which the teacher is "thrown into specific communication situations" along with the student (*Paralogic* 169). But why would anyone want a teacher thrown in unless the teacher were bringing something from a previous experience? In emphasizing the singularity of situations, Kent seeks to deny this previous experience. He cannot do so and simultaneously imagine a situation in which mentors would be of any use.

The only difference between Dewey and a postprocess, third sophistic pedagogy is that Dewey counters the will-to-system not through disruption but through experience. For Dewey, method is, at its heart, "remaking the old through union with the new" (*LSA* 50). This method is *intelligence,* which he explicitly defines as "a conversion of past experience into knowledge and projection of that knowledge in ideas and purposes that anticipate what may come to be in the future and that indicate how to realize what is desired" (50). My claim is that postpedagogy, in its current expression, has hinted at this renewal but has failed to articulate it fully. Method cannot be only a means of situated, surprising, or even disruptive invention since all situations, surprises, and disruptions are made, at least in part, out of previous situations, surprises, and disruptions. Unless we can describe this method, we have no way to "create the conditions of possibility for Acts" (Rickert, *Acts* 197).

If we are to sustain postpedagogy, we have to ask about curricular design as well as occasion design. The difficult question is not how we design the first occasion, it is how we design the next one. That is the real work—the "post" work—of postpedagogy. Dewey offers a vision for this work. Here, I discern that vision by heuristically repurposing a passage from Dewey's *Liberalism and Social Action* (1935), substituting "pedagogy" for "liberalism":

> We are always dependent upon the experience that has accumulated in the past and yet there are always new forces coming in, new needs arising, that demand, if the new forces are to operate and the new needs to be satisfied, a reconstruction of the patterns of old experience. The old and the new have forever to be integrated with each other, so that the values of old experience may become the servants and instruments of new desires and aims. We are always possessed by habits and customs, and this fact signifies that we are always influenced

by the inertia and the momentum of forces temporally out-
grown but nevertheless still present with us as a part of our
being. Human life gets set in patterns, institutional and moral. But change is also with us and demands the constant remaking of old habits and old ways of thinking, desiring and
acting. The effective ratio between the old and the stabilizing
and the new and disturbing is very different at different times.
. . . But be the ratio little or great, there is always an adjustment to be made, and as soon as the need for it becomes
conscious, [pedagogy] has a function and a meaning. It is not
that [pedagogy] creates the need, but that the necessity for
adjustment defines the office of [pedagogy]. (49)

In this argument, we find the problems that continually preoccu-
pied Dewey: the nature of experience and the role of habit and
custom versus change and renewal, along with the possibilities and
disturbances of growth. In this particular case, Dewey wonders
whether liberalism still possesses the vitality to (re)make American
politics more democratic. His fundamental argument, offered in
1935, is that liberalism has failed to make itself sufficiently historical, allowing its terminology to be repurposed in counterproductive
directions. Because it has not learned how to respond to the past,
liberalism's claims have become unmoored from any contextual
anchor. (In Burkean terms, Dewey's is an argument for casuistic
stretching more thoroughly woven into history.) As always, Dewey
is happy to express what he sees as liberalism's positive content; he
simply asserts that new events demand rearticulation of that content. Thus, we can discern some of the most ignored aspects of
Dewey's philosophy, which is that he was not a merely procedural
thinker and that he resisted the supposed division between thought
and expression. This is particularly important to remember in regard to Dewey's thoughts on education (as Russell suggests in "Vygotsky"). Dewey did not jettison "knowledge" in favor of "personal
exploration." Rather, he insisted that each needs the other as a catalyst for growth.

Meanwhile, my substitutions in the previous passage are meant
to suggest the same thing about pedagogy: "there is always an ad-

justment to be made, and as soon as the need for it becomes conscious, [pedagogy] has a function and a meaning. It is not that [pedagogy] creates the need, but that the necessity for adjustment defines the office of [pedagogy]." To be human, in Dewey's estimation, is to need to adjust our present experience to accommodate our past experience in order to serve future purposes. It is this need into which pedagogy enters. Pedagogy does not create this need; it serves this need. This reverses the "discourse of student need" that Sharon Crowley explicates in *Composition in the University*. This discourse, she argues, has little to do with students' needs, which we articulate for them, and a great deal to do with the academy's self-image (257–62). And our own self-images as professors, as those who "speak forth." As Hawk observes, too often "teachers do almost anything but listen. We plan the next question, fill in the students' answers, think about where we want to make the answers go, look for the chalk" (257–58). Dewey might call these the habits of a profession uncomfortable with uncertainty, and his entire educational philosophy is premised on the idea that we have to rewrite the learner back into that scene. Pedagogy does that by being something that responds to need, not something that imposes it. Imagine a pedagogical conversation in which we said things like, "I really responded to my students today," instead of "They really didn't respond to me today." "Begin with where they are" (Berthoff, *Making* 9), perhaps the most familiar maxim of anti-traditional pedagogy, takes on a more profound meaning. You go to them; they don't come to you. Teaching is what responds, not what elicits response. To teach—to be a professor, an academic doctor—is to be a nurse of experience. (As a son and brother-in-law of nurses, I use this term in its most honorific sense.) A Deweyan teacher helps students turn their experience-as-data into experience-as-method. This is what reflection means, and it is the most demanding pedagogical work.

Through this work, what we are after, finally, is what Dewey calls a *cultivated naïveté*:

> We cannot permanently divest ourselves of the intellectual habits we take on and wear when we assimilate the culture of

our own time and place. But intelligent furthering of culture demands that we take some of them off, that we inspect them critically to see what they are made of and what wearing them does to us. We cannot achieve recovery of primitive naïveté. But there is attainable a cultivated naïveté of eye, ear and thought, one that can be acquired only through the discipline of severe thought. (*EN* 37–38)

Pedagogy is the paradoxical work of cultivating naïveté, or what Zen practitioners call "beginner's mind." Again, the paradox: those with beginner's mind are the most experienced practitioners and the most practiced experiencers. The question of pedagogy, then, is how we ourselves cultivate the severe thought of this paradox, the severe thought required to practice experience. I mean here to avoid the discourse of student need and instead concentrate on our own need. How do we intelligently further the culture of our teaching? How do we intellectually disrobe? What would it mean to begin where we are? My answer to these questions returns to the first chapter of this book: we must make "inspired adhoccery" our habit and our hope. We must, in other words, become pedagogical casuists, a charge I explicate in the next chapter.

4

Unprincipled Pedagogy

> No principled pedagogy exists in the sense that we can stand
> outside our practices to discover a set of uncontested principles
> that will allow us to reject definitively one learning theory and to
> declare another the undisputed path to enlightenment.
>
> —Thomas Kent, "Principled Pedagogy"

> The liability of a thing to abuse is in proportion to the value of
> its right use.
>
> —John Dewey, *How We Think*

THE BUREAUCRATIZATION OF THE PEDAGOGICAL

IN *HOW WE THINK*, DEWEY COMPLAINS that the "routine formula"
of grammar and arithmetic "invades also history and even literature, which are then reduced, under plea of intellectual training,
to 'outlines,' diagrams, and schemes of division and subdivision"
(60). Having anticipated Walter Ong's analysis of Ramism, Dewey
makes what we also might call a proto-postpedagogical observation:

> The adoption by teachers of this misconception of logical
> method has probably done more than anything else to bring
> pedagogy into disrepute; for to many persons "pedagogy"
> means precisely a set of mechanical, self-conscious devices

This chapter is a revised version of a previously published article, "Unprincipled Pedagogy: Casuistry and Postprocess Teaching," in *Pedagogy*, Vol. 11, issue 2, pp. 257–283.
Copyright © 2011, Duke University Press. All rights reserved. Reprinted by permission of the present publisher, Duke University Press. www.dukeupress.edu.

for replacing by some cast-iron external scheme the personal mental movement of the individual. (60–61)

Teachers, at all levels of the curriculum, find themselves in an unenviable position: the formalistic methods by which they are asked to prove their worth are the very methods that undermine their worth. This catch-22 produces the most contemptuous and contemptible phrase in all of edu-speak: "teacher-proof curriculum." In *Practical Wisdom*, Barry Schwartz and Kenneth Sharpe observe an example of the contemporary Gradgrindian impulse in a Chicago kindergarten classroom where the teacher is doing a lesson on the letter *b*. The daily script dictates that the teacher assemble the students, give them a warning about the dangers of hot water, and then read the story *The Bath*. Unfortunately, that book is nowhere to be found, so the teacher instead reads *Jesse Bear, What Will You Wear?* In spite of this deviation, she still warns the students about the risks of taking a bath without an adult present (168). In other words, this teacher's training has incapacitated her to recognize the disconnect between her lesson and her materials. (Or perhaps her experience has capacitated her to recognize that improvisations will not be tolerated.) Little wonder, then, if the profession of teaching suffers from disrepute.

From the Deweyan perspective, postpedagogy can be understood as a call to restore the reputation of teaching as intellectual work. The basic requirement of this restoration is easy to understand but more difficult to implement. How does one expect the unexpected? If this formulation is too pat, perhaps I can put it like this: how do we practice recognizing worth that we have never before seen? In Chapter 1, I borrowed the phrase "inspired adhoccery" as a kind of aspirational statement for teaching after pedagogy. I would also suggest that inspired adhoccery is a descriptive statement. Teaching has always been work in which "solutions to particular problems will be found by regarding each situation-of-crisis as an opportunity for improvisation and not as an occasion for the application of rules and principles (although the invoking and the recharacterizing of rules and principles will often be components of the improvisation)" (Fish, *Trouble* 63–64). Perhaps the accomplishment of the postpedagogical turn will be to make composition comfortable with this sort of paradox: adhoccery can only be adhoccery because it is inspired; inspiration can only be inspiration because it is "adhocced"—that is, put into practice. Experience, in Dewey's methodical understanding, is a product of adhoccery and inspiration, which are no more separable than an organism is from its environment.

When it comes to seeing pedagogy as inspired adhoccery, we encounter what Kenneth Burke describes as "the bureaucratization of the imaginative":

> Call the possibilities "imaginative." And call the carrying-out of *one* possibility the *bureaucratization* of the imaginative. An imaginative possibility (usually at the start Utopian) is bureaucratized when it is embodied in the realities of a social texture, in all the complexity of language and habits, in the property relationships, the methods of government, production and distribution, and in the development of rituals that re-enforce the same emphasis. (*ATH* 225)[1]

Though Burke and I write about different sorts of class struggle, I nevertheless find in his description of this historical process a description of a pedagogical process. Call pedagogies "imaginative" and the carrying out of a given pedagogy the bureaucratization of the imaginative. A pedagogical possibility is bureaucratized when it is embodied in the realities of a classroom ecology. When any approach is so embodied in the realities of a social texture, in the rituals and relationships of a classroom, it risks becoming an end in itself. At some point, it is easier to insist on the bureaucratization than it is to recall the imaginative possibility that occasioned it.

According to Joseph Harris, this is what happened with process: "The advocates of process did not redirect attention to what students had to say so much as they simply argued for what seems to me a new sort of formalism—one centered no longer on textual structures but instead on various algorithms, heuristics, and guidelines for composing" (56). As we saw in Chapter 2, this particular imaginative possibility, which originally promised freedom from formal strictures, itself became a formal stricture. Like some of the postpedagogues, though, Burke might tell us not to worry too much. All bureaucratizations will eventually fail "since human beings are not a perfect fit for *any* historic texture" (*ATH* 225–26). The thousand tiny resistances mentioned by Rickert (*Acts*) will emerge regardless of any (always temporary) success at bureaucratizing. Inevitably, we will face the problem of "unintended by-products" that "become a stronger factor than the original purpose" (*ATH* 226). Process's unintended by-product turned out to be the very reductive uniformity that its initial imaginative possibility was supposed to displace.

Once this happens, Burke writes, alienation from the "reigning symbols of authority" begins to set in, though "the priests (publicists, *educators*) . . . will rebuke the opposition for its disobedience to the reigning symbols" (*ATH* 226; emphasis added). Thus, we hear reports of teachers saying, "No, no, no. . . . You can't start your rewriting until you've finished your prewriting." From a Burkean perspective, the postpedagogical argument might be read as one that reminds us not to rebuke disobedience but rather to recognize it, in both empirical and parliamentary fashion. Burke goes on to describe the circumstances under which people come to struggle against a given bureaucratic order, yet at no point does he endorse the imaginative as merely the opposite of the bureaucratic. He does not see the bureaucratic as something to be escaped, since it is the texture in which the imaginative is made manifest. Even a plan to save the world will pass through the process of bureaucratization, "thus necessarily involving elements alien to the original, 'spiritual' ('imaginative') motive" (*ATH*, Introduction 3). We should be very wary of such plans, of course; in Burke's view, the person most likely to support such plans is the devil. Yet we need *some* plans. Without risking bureaucratization, the imaginative cannot be manifested. If, as Oscar Wilde says, "[a] map of the world that does not include Utopia is not worth even glancing at" (269), an imaginative that finds no expression is not worth conjuring. We cannot place our hopes wholly in the imaginative, which, if it finds any expression at all, always occasions bureaucratization.

Characteristically, where Burke detects a poison, he also offers its antidote. His idea of "casuistic stretching," which appears in *Attitudes toward History*, suggests a way for us to inhabit the bureaucratization of the pedagogical. Through casuistic stretching, we can articulate the moments when our pedagogies become so bureaucratized that they lose their original imaginative character, or when our ad hoc inspiration devolves into "pre hoc" patterns. My argument—the payoff to which the preceding chapters have been leading—is that we can maintain this kind of "liquid attitude" (*ATH* 221) toward our pedagogy by becoming pedagogical casuists.

Admittedly, this is a tough sell. Despite some familiarity with casuistic stretching, many may not know the term *casuistry* itself, and those who do know it are likely to disdain it. While someone might be complimented for her soaring rhetoric, no one is ever complimented for his clever casuistry. Its only rival in infamy is Machiavellian *virtù*, another synonym for twisting meaning and intentions to suit ulterior motives. A list of casuistry's other common synonyms suggests why it has fallen into disuse: popery, harlotry, and—need it be said?—sophistry (Jonsen and Toulmin 11). Both Burke and Dewey, moreover, were suspicious of casuistry. Yet its biggest problem may be its obscurity rather than its infamy. Though its roots date to Cicero and its seeds to Aristotle, and though it was a central practice of moral reasoning in the Middle Ages and the Renaissance, casuistry has been forgotten since the late seventeenth century, when Pascal's *Provincial Letters*—an attack on both the Jesuit order and the casuistry Jesuits were famous for practicing—destroyed its dignity almost single-handedly. Pascal had to publish the *Letters* anonymously to avoid the wrath of the powerful Society of Jesus, but the book's impact was so great that *Escobar*, the name of a famous Jesuit casuist, "remains a synonym for 'equivocator' or 'prevaricator' in contemporary French dictionaries" (Sampson 74). Meanwhile, in English, the word *casuistry* itself found one of its earliest expressions in Alexander Pope's satiric *Rape of the Lock*, in which the "tomes of casuistry" are compared to "cages for gnats, and chains to yoke a flea" (V.121–22). As Pope's metaphors suggest, casuistry has often been seen as an excessively legalistic method of rationalization, one designed for splitting (un)ethical hairs.

Perhaps the first question is why we should turn to a practice as discredited as casuistry. Why become pedagogical casuists? The reason is that casuistry can methodize our pedagogical experience. Since Chapter 1, I have sought ways to avoid both despairing ad-hocism and rigid formalism. Obscure though it may be, arcane though it may be, casuistry offers a way to think and talk about teaching without falling into either of these traps. Yet because casuistry is obscure and arcane, here I first provide a brief but detailed historical overview. I then examine Burke's idea of casuistic stretching, along with the ways in which Dewey and Lyotard both address casuistry in their writing. Taken together, these scholars assist in articulating a method that can address the casuistic attitudes latent in postpedagogy. Finally, I close with Patricia Harkin's discussion of how composition might make a method of narrative knowledge. Though Harkin does not write about casuistry, she suggests a vision of "postdisciplinary" lore that invites a casuistic method. Casuistry, I ultimately argue, offers a means of intellectualizing practice, of speaking, writing, and thinking about teaching after pedagogy.

A BRIEF HISTORY OF (IM)PRACTICAL WISDOM

Given casuistry's reputation, it is perhaps unsurprising that the term is invoked infrequently in defenses of practical reasoning. Yet contemporary experience continues to present opportunities for casuistic intervention. In their 2010 *Practical Wisdom*, for example, Barry Schwartz and Kenneth Sharpe recount the story of a first-time offender who uses a toy gun to steal $50. The judge thinks the five-year minimum excessive and instead imposes a lighter sentence that allows the defendant to work during the day to support his family. Two years after the defendant completes his time, however, the judge is ordered to reinstate the full five-year penalty. That the defendant had no record, that he had previously earned a GED after dropping out of high school to marry his pregnant girl-friend, that he and his wife were raising their daughter, that he had been despondent over losing his job and was drunk at the time of the robbery—none of these circumstances could be taken into account (17). The rulebook said five years, regardless of circumstance.

Or consider this familiar experience, here observed by Richard Dawkins: Airport security refuses to allow a mother to carry on her daughter's eczema cream because its size is over the limit. As Dawkins notes, the security workers are bound by "the rulebook's hoops of steel," and even the suggestion that she scoop a couple of tablespoons into a jar is rejected. Stephen Toulmin relates a similar story, this one of a disabled woman living on her social security benefits who supplements her income by starting an answering service. When the social security office discovers these earnings, her benefits are reduced, putting her right back into poverty. In all of these situations, rules impose a uniformity that denies all discretion. Even when people complain about this tendency, they reveal the rule-bound psychosis. Recounting Toulmin's story, for example, a television reporter insists that "there should be a *rule* to prevent this kind of thing from happening" ("Tyranny" 32). But rules are just the problem. Though largely forgotten, casuistry offers a way of making a method of discretion.[2]

My ultimate aim, of course, is not to urge a general casuistic revival but rather a particular pedagogic revival. In this endeavor, I do have some forebears within rhetoric and composition, most notably Wayne Booth.[3] In a 2005 dialogue with Peter Elbow, Booth searched "for the hundredth time" for "a way of thinking that escapes both utter skepticism and rabid dogmatism," a way that would allow us to "assent to the validity of some values, while remembering warnings that our version of any one of them as the *only* true conception is always questionable" (Booth and Elbow 381). This sort of problem becomes more difficult when one faces a choice of competing goods or when one commitment would seem to require us to ignore another. There are situations in which "true values can genuinely clash," Booth insisted, and we may be required "to practice what Aristotle called *phronesis*, practical wisdom; what the Jesuits called casuistry" (Booth and Elbow 381).[4] As Booth suggests, casuistry is usually seen as a Machiavellian art. In spite of this reputation, however, it has never completely disappeared from discussions of moral philosophy. Most recently, it experienced a revival within medical ethics, a revival occasioned primarily by Albert Jonsen and Stephen Toulmin's 1989 *The Abuse of Casuistry.*

Jonsen and Toulmin's interest in casuistry began with their work with the National Commission for the Protection of Human Subjects of Biomedical and Behavioral Research, which was tasked by Congress with examining the ways in which human subjects were being used in research. Jonsen and Toulmin report that the eleven commission members came from a variety of backgrounds: "men and women; blacks and whites; Catholics, Protestants, Jews, and atheists; medical scientists and behaviorist psychologists; philosophers; lawyers; theologians; and public interest representatives" (17). Given this diversity, it seemed unlikely that the commissioners would find consensus on the fundamental moral issues they were facing. Yet the commission saw a way around this problem by developing taxonomies of individual cases and arranging them according to similarities and differences; "so long as the commissioners stayed on the taxonomic or casuistical level, they usually agreed in their practical conclusions" (17). Paradoxically, it was only when they offered the reasons or principles behind their recommendations that they disagreed. "If anything," writes Toulmin, "the appeal to principles undermined the recommendations by suggesting to onlookers that there was more disharmony than ever showed up in the commissioners' actual discussions" ("Tyranny" 32). Jonsen and Toulmin recognized this practice as an implicit casuistry, and this recognition led to their study of casuistry and to an intense conversation about its potential uses for medical ethical deliberation.[5]

Jonsen and Toulmin define *casuistry* as "the analysis of moral issues, using procedures of reasoning based on paradigms and analogies, leading to the formulation of expert opinions about the existence and stringency of particular moral obligations, framed in terms of rules or maxims that are general but not universal or invariable, since they hold good with certainty only in the typical conditions of the agent and the circumstances of action" (257). As an ethical practice, casuistry asks whether and when circumstances change the ways in which we judge moral action. Many readers will be familiar with such cases from undergraduate ethics courses: "Is it permissible to steal in order to avoid starving?" "Is it all right to lie in order to protect someone from harm?" Contrary to common opinion, these sorts of questions need not devolve into moral relativism, for casuists check their judgments against paradigm and analogy and frame their decisions for the particular case at hand. When Jonsen and Toulmin suggest that a casuistic solution is offered "only in the typical conditions of the agent and the circumstances of action," they mean that a judgment holds *only* for the given case. To permit lying in exceptional circumstances is not to permit lying in all circumstances.

There is not space here to assemble a full history of casuistry. Nevertheless, I want to sketch some of that history to acquaint readers and to go a little way toward recuperating casuistry's reputation. As Aristotle suggests in his foundational treatise, rhetoric's "function is concerned with the sort of things we debate and for which we do not have [other] arts" (*On Rhetoric* 1357a). Casuistry is slightly different: its purpose is to deal with things about which we deliberate when the rules seem to contradict each other. Aristotle was not a casuist, but his idea of *phronesis* reveals an awareness that rules will eventually be defied by situations. In contrast to *sophia*, *phronesis* "is about human concerns, about things open to deliberation" (*Nicomachean* 1141b). Aristotle considers ethics a species of *phronesis* rather than philosophic or theoretical wisdom because the "good" "cannot be some common and single universal; for if it were, it would be spoken of in only one [of the types of] predication, not in them all" (1096a). The good, in other words, can be understood in multiple ways, and thus our attainment of the good depends on quality, quantity, time (*kairos*), and context (1096a). Aristotle's thinking defines a wisdom for the practical realm. *Phronesis*, therefore, is not "about universals only. It must also acquire knowledge of particulars, since it is concerned with action and action is about particulars" (1141b). This knowledge about particulars requires something more than simply knowing the law:

> And so, whenever the law makes a universal rule, but in this
> particular case what happens violates the [intended scope of]
> the universal rule, on this point the legislator falls short, and

has made an error by making an unqualified rule. Then it is correct to rectify the deficiency; this is what the legislator would have said himself if he had been present there, and what he would have prescribed, had he known, in his legislation. . . . And this is the nature of the decent—rectification of law insofar as the universality of law makes it deficient. This is also the reason why not everything is guided by law. For on some matters legislation is impossible, and so a decree is needed. For the standard applied to the indefinite is itself indefinite, as the lead standard is in Lesbian building, where it is not fixed, but adapts itself to the shape of the stone; similarly, a decree is adapted to fit its objects. (*Nicomachean* 1137b)

Aristotle's analogy references a ruler he had seen on a visit to Lesbos: "A normal, straight-edged ruler was of little use to the masons who were carving round columns from slabs of stone" (Schwartz and Sharpe, *Practical* 28). So the masons bent the ruler to fit the columns. This approach seems counterintuitive: the whole point of measuring, after all, is to rely on some firm standard. Yet the carpenters of Lesbos, in addition to inventing the tape measure, recognized that certain situations demanded a more flexible standard.[6] Paradoxically, it is the universality of law that makes the law deficient. In response, practical wisdom offers the decree—a decision fit for a specific situation.

This kind of practical wisdom existed before Aristotle, of course. The *Dissoi Logoi,* perhaps the most ancient text of the Western rhetorical tradition, takes as its basic assumption that every issue has at least two views. Death "is bad for those who die, but good for the undertakers and grave-diggers" (Bizzell and Herzberg 48). The text observes the same dichotomies for a number of other experiences and practices: food, drink, sex, illness, farming, trading, etc. The effect of these contrasting arguments is that one can understand ethical behavior only from the perspective of a given situation. Medicine, interestingly enough, offers the author of the *Dissoi Logoi* a productive example: "For if it were necessary that one's father or mother should consume some medicament (whether in solid or liquid form), but he or she was unwilling, is it not just to give them the medicament in their food or in their drink and not say that it is in it? So it is already clear that it is just to tell lies and to deceive one's parents" (Bizzell and Herzberg 51). In this case, we see the basic outlines of casuistic thought: there is a principle that normally should not be violated, yet there is a particular case that defies deductive application of the principle. The result is that what seems unjust suddenly seems just under the given circumstances.

In addition to anticipating certain problems in medical ethics, this example anticipates what would become the central question of casuistry: are there situations in which it is permissible, or perhaps even desirable, to do what is expedient rather than what is honorable? In his *De Officiis,* or *On Duties* (44 BC), the third book of which is considered to be the first formal casuistic manual, Cicero wrestles with this very question. As the date suggests, Cicero had recently faced the very real casuistic problem of the assassination of Julius Caesar. Though Cicero had not participated in the plot, he retroactively approved of it on the grounds that Caesar had become a tyrant: "Did the beneficial, therefore, overcome honorableness? No indeed, for honorableness followed upon what benefited" (III.19). Throughout *On Duties,* Cicero considers examples of cases in which "one might deliberate not whether to abandon honorableness because the benefit is great (for that is certainly wicked); but rather whether it may be possible to do that which seems beneficial in a way that is not dishonorable" (III.39). Regarding truth telling, he offers several paradigm cases, some dealing with honor in business, others with honor in war:

> For example, suppose that a good man had brought a large quantity of corn from Alexandria to Rhodes at a time when corn was extremely expensive among the Rhodians because of shortage and famine. If he also knew that several more merchants had set sail from Alexandria, and had seen their boats *en route* laden with corn and heading for Rhodes, would he tell the Rhodians? Or would he keep silent and sell his own produce at as high a price as possible? (III.50)[7]

Cicero then imagines a debate between his various sources, maintaining all the while that one cannot do what is expedient if it is dishonorable. Expediency is permissible, in other words, if it avoids dishonor. He suggests that concealment is not dishonorable in and of itself, but it is dishonorable to profit by someone else's ignorance (III.57). But there are situations in which such concealment is permissible. If one is captured by pirates in war and makes some promise in order to be set free, it is permissible to break this promise because pirates are not worthy of our good faith. To lie to a worthy enemy, however, is a different matter: Cicero praises Marcus Atilius Regulus, a Roman captive of Carthage who was allowed to return home to negotiate for the release of Carthaginian prisoners on the condition that he return if his mission failed. When he arrived in Rome, he insisted that Rome keep the prisoners as it was in her best interest. Then Regulus kept his promise and returned to Carthage to face death (III.99–112). It is not permissible to say, "I swore with my tongue; I have kept my mind unsworn" (Euripides, qtd. in Cicero III.108). This practice would later come to be known as "mental reservation," in which a person answers a question with the partial truth rather than the full. Some casuists would reserve mental reservation for mundane situations such as telling someone at the door that your spouse is not at home when he or she really is. "No (not for you)" is the suggested answer. But there have been much more dire circumstances for exercising mental reservation, as when members of one church faced questioning from members of another church (particularly during the Reformation and Counter-Reformation).

Several centuries after Cicero, casuistry would find its way into Roman Catholic moral and legal philosophy when the *Digest* of Justinian was rediscovered in 1070. Earlier scholars had believed Roman law to be more of a code than a collection of cases; they now saw that the so-called code was intensely casuistic. As a result of this influence, canon lawyers were disposed toward *aequitas* and Aristotelian *epieikeia* (both words for what we call "equity"), and canon law itself became "preeminently a practical discipline" (Jonsen and Toulmin 116). This practical approach to human affairs later manifested itself in the Church's confessional practice, which trained confessors to apply the complexities of canon law to particular cases (117–18). Confession depended on the particular situation of the person seeking absolution. Confessional casuistry would become even more important during the Reformation and Counter-Reformation. After the Council of Trent in the mid-sixteenth century, the penitent was obliged through confession "to expiate the circumstances, which alter the nature of the sin, because otherwise, one cannot judge of the weight of the Excesses, and impose a condign Punishment" (Sarpi, qtd. in Sampson 77). Guiding the penitent was not a matter of conveying adamantine moral principles but rather of discerning possible resolutions.

The discussion of alternative possibilities was a central feature of Jesuit casuistry during its high period of 1556–1656, a period that saw the emergence of the Society of Jesus as the Church's most prominent casuists. The Jesuits' historical context made them ideally suited for casuistry. Jesuit historian John O'Malley writes that the Jesuits sought to "accommodate to circumstances and to the particular needs and situation of the persons to whom [they] ministered" (81). Ignatius, the founder of the Jesuits, insisted that Jesuit confessors observe "each person's temperament and character" and begin conversations "with subjects of interest to the other, so that with a merchant one spoke of trade. A Spanish proverb quoted often by Ignatius suggested 'going in by their door to come out by ours'" (O'Malley 112). The Jesuits *Ratio Studiorum*, the curriculum by which they administered their worldwide system of education, includes "Rules for the Professor of Cases of Conscience," designed for the professor training parish priests in the art of confessing. The teacher was to present cases to his students for their consideration, and he was enjoined to "confirm his own opinions in such a way that, if there is any other opinion that can be approved and that is supported by reputable authors, he should indicate that it too can be approved" (sec. 201). As this passage suggests, casuists assumed that more than one opinion could be plausibly accepted.[8]

If the impression of scarlet-clad, mustache-twirling Jesuits is what has survived of casuistry's high period, the praise or blame can be attributed largely to Blaise Pascal, whose 1656 *Provincial Letters* more or less did to casuistry what Ramus did to rhetoric. Pascal had been recruited to write a defense of the Jansenists, the Jesuits' most serious theological opponents in seventeenth-century France. Indeed, to defend the Jansenists was to attack the Jesuits, a task that Pascal pursued enthusiastically. The book's central conceit is a dialogue between a worldly Jesuit father and a devout naïf, played by Pascal himself. His anonymous alter ego simply asks the Jesuit questions, and the priest happily and imprudently provides honest answers. Open the *Letters* to almost any page and one finds a blistering and hilarious critique of the dangers of casuistry. In Letter VI, for example, Pascal and the Jesuit discuss a recent ruling that allows monks to avoid excommunication when they remove their habits upon entering a gambling hall or brothel, or when they pick pockets:

> "The popes have denounced excommunication on monks who lay aside their canonicals; our casuists, notwithstanding, put it as a question, 'On what occasions may a monk lay aside his religious habits without incurring excommunication?' They mention a number of cases in which he may, and among others the following: 'If he has laid it aside for an infamous purpose, such as to pick pockets or go *incognito* into haunts of profligacy, meaning shortly after to resume it. . . .'"
>
> I could hardly believe that. . . . "And why, father," I asked, "are they discharged from excommunication on such occasions?"
>
> "Don't you understand it?" he replied. "Only think what a scandal it would be, were a monk surprised in such a predicament with his canonicals on!" (389–90)

Though Pascal lost the immediate battle—the Jansenists eventually disappeared while the Jesuits endured (at least until the eighteenth century)—he managed to win the war. By the late seventeenth century, the Holy See condemned the laxness found in casuistical literature (Jonsen and Toulmin 270). Meanwhile, the general cultural climate was turning against prudential, practical reasoning. With the advent of Galileo and Descartes (interestingly, a student of the Jesuits), "the European intellectual world was entranced by the ideas of 'system' and 'method'" (Jonsen and Toulmin 275). That focus on system and method would de-emphasize particular circumstances. In *Cosmopolis,* Toulmin writes, "From 1600 on . . . most philosophers are committed to questions of abstract, universal theory, to the exclusion of such concrete issues" (24). As the Enlightenment took shape, casuistry's fate was sealed. Moral philosophy began to seek surer ground. Both Kant (1724–1804) and Comte (1798–1857) contributed to this shift: Kant was "looking for a supreme principle upon which to ground moral law," and Comte went even further and tried to create a "social physics" by which society could be organized with something approaching scientific certainty (Tallmon, "Casuistry and the Role" 379–80). Toulmin seconds this reading of Kant, writing that "his emphasis on universal moral maxims extends into ethics an ideal of 'rationality' that had been formulated by Descartes, in logic and natural philosophy, more than a century before" (*Cosmopolis* 8). As a result of all these factors, the practical art of casuistry gradually slipped into obscurity.

CASUISTRY AND CLASSROOM ETHICS

Through this brief history, I hope I have managed to salvage casuistry's reputation at least a little. Rhetoricians have recuperated words such as *sophistry, prudence,* and, of course, *rhetoric* itself. Surely there is room for *casuistry.* But more than family resemblances are at stake. Teaching is first and foremost an ethical act, as Anne Frances Wysocki points out:

> The murmuring background soundtrack to all our work sings that it is ethics, it is always ethics, within every reddened marginal correction we make, every request for another draft, every discussion about the social embeddedness and articulations of writing and composing. It is all about ethics in the oldest sense because we are trying, with those actions, to shape what we are to value. (282)

Moreover, the ethics of teaching demands casuistry. A student asks for an extension. "I am swamped in my other classes," she says.

This claim (which students invariably fail to understand insults the teacher to whom they are talking) might not win much sympathy, until we consider that the student (a) has never missed a deadline, (b) has been stellar all semester long, (c) is holding down a full-time job, (d) is raising three kids alone, and (e) is a member of the honor society. Given these circumstances, teachers might be inclined to bend the rules a bit. This is a basic casuistic situation, in which circumstances seem to demand some deviation from the usual procedure.

The teacher continues to develop casuistic habits with the next case. Say, for example, that during the following semester, another student asks for an extension. In this case, it is the stereotypic FYC lost cause: a smirking, eye-rolling, slouching, arms-folding, backwards-baseball-cap-wearing student (recalcitrant students always wear baseball caps) who shuffles to the lectern and says, "My frat is having a pledge event and I need an extension." Compared to the single-mother Rhodes scholar, our resistant pupil may have less of a chance of winning us over. But further investigation might also reveal that the pledge event is a service project and that the student suffers from alopecia. In that case, we might be willing to see enough similarities in the situations to grant an extension to the second student as well. Even if we concede that one appellant is far more worthy of consideration than the other, we are practicing casuistry, albeit informally. We have recognized that a particular case defies the usual way of proceeding; we compare our reading of the present case to our experience in previous cases; we make a judgment that pertains only to the case at hand. This last move is crucial. Casuistry does not change the rules based on a single situation. It offers a temporary exception that will evaporate when the specific circumstances evaporate. Thus, we no longer need to invoke that all-too-common and self-contradicting mantra of the moral rigorist: "If I give you special treatment, I have to give everyone special treatment." If treatment is special, by its own definition it cannot be given to everyone. Casuistry allows us to articulate reasons why Baseball Cap may not warrant the same consideration as Rhodes Scholar. "But you gave her an extension" is an argument that works only if the two cases share sufficient and relevant similarity.

More important than a trivial case of classroom management are the cases in which a piece of writing demands special consideration. In composition, the most perplexing cases tend to emerge from student work, especially student work that defies our normal habits of evaluation and response. It is easy to deal with a paper that consistently fails according to some easily measurable criteria. No sources? No thesis statement? No paragraphs? Check, check, check. It is harder, however, to respond to a paper that fails in some measurable way but still manages to do something interesting or compelling. The writing may have no sources, but the style may be so arresting that we put down the red pen as we read. These are the kinds of situations to which postpedagogy wants to be sensitive. In fact, the entire postpedagogical project hinges on being sensitive to these situations. Again we might look at Rickert's Act, which suggests the way in which the imaginative butts up against the bureaucratized. Praising Pierce's writing, Rickert writes that "the paper matters to the extent that it has borne fruit and achieved a social effect" (*Acts* 197). The paper has disrupted the familiar classroom economy of value, and therefore it must be taken more on its own terms rather than on preset terms. Of course, this choice is not absolute: our recognition of unusual work is predicated on our ability to describe usual work. But, as with casuistry, postpedagogy insists that one must *begin* with the particular case at hand.

The postpedagogical teacher faces the equivalent of what Dewey calls a "moral situation." For Dewey, a moral situation is not simply a situation in which we act morally according to a standard; rather, it is a situation in which we are faced with a challenge to our usual habits of deliberation. When the ends of an action are taken for granted, there is no moral situation as Dewey understands it. At one time, for example, eating a fast-food cheeseburger would not have been considered a moral (or immoral) act insofar as few gave it a second thought. In the early days of fast food, we had not yet invented the kind of industrial systems that are cruel to humans, animals, and environment alike. But today, when we know more about the suffering of animals, the environmental harm caused by industrially produced beef, the labor abuses that so often occur during slaughter and processing, and the health costs of meat consumption, eating a fast-food cheeseburger can easily become a moral act—that is, an act with moral import. We know that a better choice must be made, but perhaps we have not developed the habits necessary to making it. In *Ethics*, coauthored with James Tufts, Dewey writes, "Conduct as moral may thus be defined as *activity called forth and directed by ideas of value or worth, where the values concerned are so mutually incompatible as to require consideration and selection before an overt action is entered upon*" (194).[9] This description is casuistic in that it sees ethics as growing out of situations in which our own values confront one another: "Let the value of one proposed end be felt to be really incompatible with that of another, let it be felt to be so opposed as to appeal to a different kind of interest and choice, in other words, to different kinds of disposition and agency, and we have a moral situation" (Dewey and Tufts 192). From this perspective, Rickert's Act occasions a "moral situation" that demands that we reconsider our usual habits of response. When—like Bartholomae reading Quentin Pierce's paper—we do not quite know what to do, we are in the pedagogical equivalent of a moral situation, or what we might call the "pedagogical situation."

In addition to seeing the pedagogical situation as one of clashing values, postpedagogy reveals other casuistic tendencies. In her ideal classroom, for example, Diane Davis endorses a "black-market economy," an idea she borrows from Susan Jarratt. In this classroom economy, "students would be invited to explore the *excesses* in their language that can't be contained by the strictures and structures of the 'old economy'" (246). Students are encouraged to let their writing "respond to its own call" rather than being bound by the strictures of the academy or a discourse community or any prefab rubric. When teachers encounter such excesses—surprising moments of insight, beauty, or possibility—they "might be able to cut under-the-table 'deals' with their students" (246). That is, they come up with some alternate way of accepting and accounting for the writing that has exceeded the intentions or parameters of the class:

Here's an example: A student drops a word, writes a brilliant fragment in a journal, a daily assignment, a part of the paper that doesn't fit. I say, This is really interesting. Why don't you go with this? . . . The student says, Will it count? . . . And I say, Well . . . it doesn't really fit an assignment, but . . . we'll cut a deal, a special deal. [But] you, the teacher, can't announce this as your plan, your intent to the whole class without falling back into the old economy. (Jarratt, qtd. in Davis 246)[10]

This description captures a casuistic situation. There is some "law" (i.e., an assignment, let's say with a rubric). A student has written something compelling, interesting, beautiful, but in a way that defies that law. The teacher is faced with a difficult choice. She may impose her rubric and fail the paper, which serves the rubric but not the student. Imagine, for example, grading Quentin Pierce on a standard-issue evaluation. ("I see a thesis here, 'Man is an asshole,' but I don't see any secondary support. Did you go to the library like I suggested?") A naive student might simply be convinced that he can't write; a more cynical—but no less sincere—student like Quentin might be permanently alienated from school. Alternatively, the teacher can ignore the rubric and, following Jarratt, construct some other way of appreciating the paper's power. This may also seem like a bad option. Presumably, I've taken some time to fashion a good assignment and an appropriate means of evaluation. Now I'm supposed to throw it away? No, says the casuist (and Jarratt). You suspend it for *this* student and *this* assignment. In fact, you concentrate so particularly on this student that you don't tell anyone else. It may be that many other students succeeded or failed at the assignment on its own terms. For most of them, the law may well serve. Casuistry is for the student whom the law does not serve, the student whose work—at least at that particular moment—seems to make us choose between being attentive to her specific needs on the one hand and supporting the curriculum we have designed on the other. (Specificity may appear more inviting than curriculum; the former echoes the imaginative and the latter bureaucracy. But if we have carefully designed our occasions, following through on the curriculum is just as important as being on the lookout for surprise.)

The casuistic tendencies of postpedagogy should not be surprising. Lyotard—whose notion of paralogy has occasioned the entire postpedagogical project—recognizes the need for casuistry in his and Jean-Loup Thébaud's *Just Gaming*. Lyotard also recognizes that ethical obligations "are never grounded: one can never reach the just by a conclusion" (17). Judgment "does not hang upon the observance of criteria" (17). Interestingly, Lyotard derives his model—or nonmodel—of judgment not from the sophists but from Aristotle's *Rhetoric* and *Ethics*: "A judge worthy of the name has no true model to guide his judgments, and therefore prescriptions, just so, without criteria. This is, after all, what Aristotle calls prudence. It consists in dispensing justice without models" (26). Rickert's idea of the Act presumes this same position. The job of pedagogy is not so much to elicit this kind of work, but rather to make prudential judgments about how to respond to it. There is no way to front-load these judgments, no way to write them into a rubric ("10% for spelling; 20% for MLA; 30% for excess and desire").

Davis, however, takes Jarratt's black-market idea a step further and imagines a classroom "in which the economy is *always* dark, shifting, erupting, out of order; in which there is no safe place to rest or to catch one's breath" (246). In Davis's classroom, the black-market economy would be *the* economy: all inspiration, all imaginative. Following the logic of Burke's paradox of purity, I wonder whether the purely imaginative can finally be imaginative at all (*GM* 35). Davis's inclination is understandable. If the black-market economy is where we find the excitement, why not stay there? Whatever response we offer, the black-market economy is also a bureaucratization, one that might become as brittle as the formal economy it was meant to disrupt. What happens when, struggling to catch her breath, a student resists this black-market economy with a really strong thesis-support argument against euthanasia? Or a five-paragraph essay that, say, demolishes some commonplace on either side of the abortion debate? An entirely black-market economy does not know what to do with these papers any more than Bartholomae's standard economy knew what to do with Quentin Pierce's. Postpedagogical method wants the "accident," but seeking it undermines its surprise. The question, then, is how we might construct a method that would negotiate the tension between the bureaucratization and the imaginative. We cannot substitute an illegitimate economy for a legitimate one. Instead, we have to discern the way a particular piece of writing relates to either. My argument is that a casuistic practice—not to say "economy," which would cancel out the possibility of casuistry—can maintain the necessary liquid pedagogical attitude.

"Liquid attitude" is another phrase I borrow from Burke, whose notion of "casuistic stretching" describes one way to live with and within the bureaucratization of the imaginative. In casuistic stretching, Burke writes, "one introduces new principles while theoretically remaining faithful to old principles" (*ATH* 229). Through this practice of metaphorical extension, we come to associate an old term with a new set of meanings. "Thus," writes Burke, "we saw the church permitting the growth of investment in a system of law that explicitly forbade investment" (229). Burke here refers to the casuistic stretch that shifted the meaning of "loaning at interest" to "loaning at risk," which allowed the Church to reconcile its teaching with new mercantile economies.[11] While this may seem to modern readers like a case of ecclesiastical hypocrisy, it can also be seen as an attempt to articulate the spirit of a law within the exigence of a new letter. Casuistry, in other words, is the imaginative become bureaucratized. "One could think of the Grammatical resources as *principles*, and of the various philosophies as *casuistries* which apply these principles to temporal situations" (*GM* xvi). Burke himself distinguishes casuistic stretching from "opportunism," the latter of which he defines as casuistic stretching "without a sufficiently broad rationale and sufficiently sophisticated methodology to make it positive" (306). Opportunism is casuistry in the worst sense of the word; it is a "shift in *policy*, not matched by a broadening in *perspective*" (*ATH* 306). Opportunism makes an exception to solve a problem; casuistic stretching makes an exception within an ongoing praxis whose risks "must be transcended by the explicit conversion of a method into a methodology" (232). By making casuistry "*absolute* and *constant*" (230), we can not only check opportunism, but also make a sort of jurisprudence out of our pedagogical experience.[12] Jurisprudence is a system not of law or code but of articulating and rearticulating experience. Rickert hints at this kind of casuistic understanding in a suggestive reference to Deleuze: "'It's jurisprudence, ultimately, that creates law. . . . Writers ought to read law reports rather than the civil code'" (*Acts* 197). This is a casuistic conception of the development of law, which does not operate simply as a set of rules but instead as an ongoing accretion of cases.[13] The law is produced by casuistic stretching. Lyotard makes a similar comment in *Just Gaming*: "One works 'case by case' even when one is producing a constitution; after all, it can only be implemented in the light of practice" (Lyotard and Thébaud 28). My argument resembles Lyotard's (and Rickert's): when the question is pedagogy, one works case by case because pedagogy can be implemented only in the light of practice.

Most important, an absolute and constant casuistic stretching can help us arrive at those moments when our bureaucratizations are stretched too far: "The devices for ostensibly retaining allegiance to an 'original principle' by casuistic stretching eventually lead to demoralization, which can only be stopped by a new start" (Burke, *ATH* 229). In other words, there comes a point in any casuistry where the stretch can no longer reach. We thus arrive at "perspective by incongruity," which "interprets new situations by removing words from their 'constitutional' setting" (309). Tables and chairs, Burke writes, go together in our world. If an artist wants us to see a table and chair differently, he has to add elements that are not conventionally there, elements that would seem incongruous and therefore offer "interpretive ingredients" (311). Burke also suggests that incongruities can be moral, which suggests a resemblance to Dewey's idea of the moral situation—that is, one in which some incongruous element or elements rewrite the scene. Again, I think of fast food, perhaps an image of a nuclear family sitting at the plastic table and on the plastic chairs of a hamburger chain. Burke's artist might add a maimed slaughterhouse worker sitting at the next table, thus occasioning perspective on this otherwise benign vision of family life. Or perhaps he would create an image reminiscent of Rockwell's iconic *Thanksgiving* in order to casuistically stretch an ideal of the family meal. Burke argues, "We contend that 'perspective by incongruity' makes for a *dramatic* vocabulary, with weighting and counter-weighting, in contrast with the liberal ideal of *neutral* naming in the characterization of processes" (311). (We see this liberal ideal in composition's own characterization of processes as *the* process.) Lyotard also recognizes the drama of casuistry: "What does Greek mythology let us see? A society of gods that is constantly forced to redraw its code" (Lyotard and Thébaud 17).

When a stretch has become demoralized—when the old wineskin can no longer hold the new wine—"perspective by incongruity" "is designed to 'remoralize' by accurately naming a situation already demoralized by inaccuracy" (Burke, *ATH* 308–9). When such a situation is renamed, we can reanimate language and ideas that have lost their elasticity. Casuistic stretching need not be merely a trick for rationalization through misnomer; it can also afford opportunities to reinvent methods that have run their course. This claim counters the common assumption that casuistry (like rhetoric, like sophistry) is a gateway drug to ethical anarchy. This worry presumes that a foundation is somewhere available. But as Burke notes, language (and the moral systems it produces) comes from liquid, even when is has cooled and hardened. "Let one of these crusted distinctions return to its source, and in this alchemic center it may be remade, again becoming molten liquid, and may enter into new combinations, whereat it may be again thrown forth as a new crust, a different distinction" (*GM* xix). Dramatism—which uses casuistry to apply Burke's grammar to particular situations—can return language and morals to their alchemic centers. It offers "a firmer kind of certainty, though it lack[s] the deceptive comforts of ideological rigidity" (*ATH* 231). This is not to say that Burke unreservedly endorses casuistry, as we have seen. But he also believes that casuistic stretching is unavoidable: "Since language owes its very existence to casuistry, casuistic stretching is beyond all possibility of 'control by elimination'" (230). As with rhetoric, we can pretend that we're not doing it and do it badly, or we can do it openly and perhaps do it better. Nevertheless, as with rhetoric, there is no guarantee that we will do it better. Thus Lyotard writes, in what strikes me as a very Burkean statement: "And so, when the question of what justice consists in is raised, the answer is: 'It remains to be seen in each case,' and always in humor, but also in worry, because one is never certain that one has been just, or that one can ever be just" (Lyotard and Thébaud 99). The comic frame so central to Burke's thought is also crucial to casuistry. For Burke, the comic frame sees "people not as *vicious*, but as *mistaken*" (*ATH* 41). Comedy is the "attitude of attitudes," which mediates the bureaucratization of the imaginative, the "process of processes" (*ATH* 3). The stretchings of casuistry may sometimes be ridiculous, but their very ridiculousness is what allows our deliberations to proceed in humor. Our failures, in other words, need not *only* worry us.

TOWARD PEDAGOGIC STRETCHING

The question, then, is what pedagogical casuistry might finally look like. To sketch a casuistry for composition, I turn not to law but to medical ethics, an arena of deliberation that also rejects the idea that "the chiaroscuro of our moral experience can be reduced to one or two overarching sources of moral values, such as maximization of happiness or respect for human freedom. While such an assumption is likely to please theorists bent upon achieving simplicity and efficiency, it will not do justice to the rich diversity inherent in the moral lives of individuals in societies" (Arras, "Principles" 990). In response to the particularity of situation, medical ethicists have appealed to casuistry in search of a case-based method.[14] In "Casuistry as Methodology in Clinical Ethics," Jonsen describes how a medical casuistry proceeds through three basic moves: morphology, taxonomy, and kinetics. By *morphology*, Jonsen refers to the initial interpretation of the "interplay of circumstances and maxims" that "constitute the structure of a case" (299). That is, morphology begins by trying to figure out what is happening in a given case. "*In hoc casu* is the constant refrain" (Arthos 333). Being *in hoc*, however, also means owing something to our experience. Because we cannot treat a case, or a situation, as a discrete entity—as though it could be divorced from experience—we interpret the case according to maxims, rules of thumb that guide (but do not deduce) decision-making. For example, a casuist might interpret a case of self-defense according to the maxim *vim vi repellere*, or "force may be repulsed by force" (Jonsen and Toulmin 253). The appeal to this maxim does not necessarily settle the question at hand, but it does open some possibilities and close others.

Though composition has not made a habit of articulating rules of thumb as such, there are those who have offered maxims for our work. Berthoff, for example, includes a series of such maxims in the first chapter of *The Making of Meaning* (9–12):

> Begin with where they are.
>
> How you construe is how you construct.
>
> To understand is to invent. (Jean Piaget)
>
> Elements of what we want to end with must be present in some form from the start.
>
> To the teacher, the simplest and most general appears the easiest, whereas for a pupil only the complex and living appears easy. (Leo Tolstoy)

Whether or not we endorse these particular maxims, they suggest some way to import our experience into new pedagogical situations without imposing our experience on the new situations. Where students are will vary from situation to situation. Paulo Freire's nonliterate Brazilian peasants, the example Berthoff offers (9–10), are not first-year composition students in the United States. Nevertheless, beginning with where our students are might help us avoid the perils of recipe swapping: "You hear something described that sounds good; it's obviously foolproof; you try it, and it doesn't work. So you feel terrible" (*Making* 34). As you try to figure out what is going wrong, or where the difficulty lies with your teaching (rather than with your students), the maxim may help rearticulate experience for the new situation. Again, we are after the spirit of the law rather than the letter. Why have Freirean applications not always fared well in North American composition classrooms? Without a conscious casuistic stretch from Freire's situation to our own—a stretch that can be articulated through maxims as simple as "begin with where they are"—transplanted pedagogies are far less likely to flourish.

Jonsen lists *taxonomy*, or "the lining up of cases in a certain order" ("Casuistry as Methodology" 301), as the next step of casuistry. As we see with maxims, case analysis is always conditioned by experience, which is produced in part by comparison to previous "paradigm" cases. The maxims of morphology are the product of our experience. Casuistic taxonomy represents an attempt to make the dialectical relationship between the given and the new as explicit (as absolute and constant) as possible. If the question of morphology echoes the stasis question of conjecture, the question of taxonomy begins to move the stasis discussion toward definition. We answer the definition question through taxonomic comparison: how is the case like previous cases, and how is it unlike them? Through this questioning, casuists hope to better discern what is particularly important about the present problem. We understand the baseball-capped frat boy through the experience of understanding the single-mother Rhodes scholar. Taxonomy makes that deliberation explicit. The risk of taxonomy, from a paralogic perspective, is that it sounds excessively systemic. During the era of high casuistry, for example, casuists produced "immense, elaborate volumes filled with minute distinctions and detailed, sometimes contorted, arguments . . . reminiscent of the art and architecture of the Baroque era" (Jonsen and Toulmin 145). The complexity of these volumes, however, reflected the complexity of moral experience.[15] This development is organic: there is a logic to it, but the shapes and connections produced by that logic cannot be predicted with accuracy. Neither Procrustean or Protean, casuistic taxonomy balances the influence of the given against the data of the new.

Casuistry tempers the idea of taxonomy with Jonsen's third step, *kinetics*. By "kinetics," Jonsen refers not to linear movement, but rather to "the way in which one case imparts a kind of moral movement to other cases, as a moving billiard ball imparts motion to the stationary one it hits" ("Casuistry as Methodology" 303). In casuistry, "a case can so depart from precedent as to establish its own category" (Arthos 333). Kinetics tries to determine the direction in which Burke's molten liquid is flowing: "In this view of things, understanding is organic, like the deposits of coral on the sea shelf that build whole geological structures over time" (Arthos 333). The movement, or development, of one case changes the position of the other cases on whose wisdom we might draw. In other words, the casuist practices a Deweyan reflection on experience, one in which the past reshapes our understanding of the present, but the present also reshapes our understanding of the past. The order produced by this bivalent movement is not efficient. It develops as a network rather than as a grid. Like the "moment of complexity" that Mark Taylor describes in his book of that name, the kinetic taxonomy of casuistry falls "*between* order and chaos" and "is the point at which self-organizing systems emerge to create new patterns of coherence and structures of relation" (24). There is what we might call a "coral order" to the casuistic taxonomy, one that unfolds neither as pure system nor as pure surprise.

The role of taxonomy is perhaps the most counterintuitive move both for composition and for the argument I've made so far in these pages. As rhetoricians, we are used to focusing on the specifics of a particular situation, so the case focus of casuistry likely seems acceptable. Maxims, moreover, may be intuitively persuasive, even if we have not explicitly considered them in the way we teach. I suspect that most experienced teachers could quickly offer rules of thumb by which they navigate particular kinds of situations. If nothing else, it might make sense for us as a field to follow Berthoff in articulating the maxims that guide our practice. But the second step of casuistry, taxonomy, may conjure Foucauldian anxieties about various and insidious micropolitical expressions of power. That the kinetic and constant rearrangement of these taxonomies suggests a network rather than a hierarchy may not be entirely reassuring. If taxonomy makes us uneasy, we might reframe the concept as *repertoire*. Donald Schön writes, "The practitioner has built up a *repertoire* of examples, images, understandings, and actions. . . . A practitioner's repertoire includes the whole of his experience insofar as it is accessible to him for understanding and action. When a practitioner makes sense of a situation he perceives to be unique, he *sees* it *as* something already present in his repertoire" (*Reflective* 138). This statement captures the seeming paradox at the heart of casuistry: we see something as unique because we see it through the repertoire of experience. We know surprise by knowing the familiar.

The problem is simple, even trite: you learn to teach by teaching. Like Shakespeare, I hate to resort to cliché, but in this case, what else is there? What other maxim could express the paradox of pedagogical experience? You learn to teach by teaching. No doubt, more formal empirical methods produce vital information. I also share Richard Fulkerson's concern ("Epistemic," examined in Chapter 1) that qualitative methods may become so dominant that they wipe out any hint of epistemological diversity. Yet the rigor of such studies can only really be tested within an actual classroom. In other words, to say that a formal study is more reliable than a piece of lore leaves all our work still to be done. Any piece of information I bring to the classroom, no matter its source, has to undergo the main test, and we will still need a method of understanding our successes and our failures. A more systematic approach to classroom experience—that is, a casuistry for teaching—would allow us to claim the benefits of lore (particularity, specificity) without the detriments of lore (vacillation, solipsism). What I am urging, then, is not an uncritical embrace of lore. A casuistic analysis problematizes (in the Freirean sense) a naive reliance on "I did such-and-such, and the kids seemed to love it."

As Berthoff has pointed out, the problem with this type of storytelling is not the story itself. (It is no more critical to mistrust our experience than it is naive to trust it.) The problem is that the storytelling of lore never encounters a method by which we might challenge its claims. In this regard, Fulkerson is absolutely right. Without some method, there is no way to gauge a particular lore claim. Therefore, he offers a cautionary representative anecdote in which a teacher tries to train her students to remember handbook rules by requiring that they write them five times for every paper error ("Epistemic" 47–48). As Fulkerson does not even need to suggest, most compositionists would recoil at this approach. But how, he asks, do we justify our reaction without recourse to some kind of epistemology, an epistemology that would seem to undermine the "loreness" of lore? How do we say that we know that's wrong without going outside of lore? Yet the move outside of lore risks losing the particularity and complexity of experience. It is easy to imagine a different piece of lore that seems plausible even if it is not susceptible to scientific testing. Lore, for example, might offer a defense for the teaching of formal argument, an endeavor that Fulkerson endorses but that has become somewhat unfashionable in the field. I would be hesitant to dismiss a traditionalist's assertion that his students benefit from arguments about abortion and capital punishment until I had heard more about the experience. But neither do I think that a teacher, searching for ways to engage the particular students she has in her classroom, needs to justify every choice with empirical data.

At the heart of the problem of lore lies a difficult choice. Either lore becomes something other than it is in order to be properly validated as knowledge, or it remains lore and is never recognized as knowledge. The problem, moreover, can be nearly impossible to speak about. It is all too easy to find oneself writing things like, "I am not saying that lore should never be submitted to *more formal/ rigorous/empirical* discipline." Our very language seems prone to suggesting that lore is "informal" or "softer" or "haphazard." These distinctions imply that lore has to be translated into some other form before we can rely on it. North makes this very claim in *The Making of Knowledge in Composition*. Even while he appears to endorse lore as legitimate for practice, he rejects the possibility that it might be seen as scholarship. To write up lore, he argues, is to offer "the stylized monologue with a vengeance" (53). Stories of teaching experience "can be entertaining, even inspiring," but they should not be "mistaken for reality" (52). They may be fine for the hallway or the break room, maybe even in a conference setting, but writing these stories as a type of knowledge misrepresents what they are. Since practitioners compete for space with "Scholars" and "Researchers," writes North, "Practitioner knowledge very often gets presented with some of the trappings of Scholars' or Researchers' inquiry, with confusion on both sides over just what is being offered" (53). This is a danger, particularly for beginning teachers: "For new practitioners, especially, the Monday morning confrontation between visionary inspiration and who-shows-up can hurt" (52).

Once again, we stumble upon the Monday Morning Question: what happens when I try to *do* with what I *know?* North, it seems to me, does not offer much evidence that lore will have any more trouble answering this question than any other form of knowledge. Surely there is just as much danger from a teacher who is so thoroughly convinced by a quantitative empirical study that he cannot adjust to his students. Moreover, while I agree with many of my fellow compositionists that literature is not the be-all and end-all of human experience, I am disturbed by North's Socratic dismissal of narrative knowledge. Not only does he mistrust writing, but he also would ban poets from his ideal republic. No doubt all teachers have had the experience of running a particular play they've borrowed from somebody else, only to watch it fall apart on the field. That failure, however, is not the fault so much of teacherly literature as it is a lack of teacherly literary criticism. It is true: we do not need a generation of teachers who, having seen *Dead Poets Society* one too many times, charge into the classroom like some pedagogical Don Quixote. But that danger should be ameliorated not by dismissing teachers' experience as mere storytelling but rather by making a method of that storytelling. Otherwise, we are left with North's depressing notion of a false "visionary inspiration" that can only be disappointed by the "who-shows-up." (Impervious to visionary inspiration, the who-shows-up are apparently eager for data-driven instruction.) Meanwhile, North's distinction entirely ignores the lessons of pragmatism. (It turns out that Dewey might not quite be *everywhere* in our work.) In North's mind, practice and philosophy are two different endeavors, and to connect them is to undermine them.

Patricia Harkin tries to avoid these false choices in her 1991 "The Postdisciplinary Politics of Lore." Though this piece does not mention either John Dewey or casuistry, it offers the best possibility for articulating the uses of experience for composition. Harkin does an impressive job of dodging the binaries that reduce lore to tall tales told around a Xerox machine. Her distinction is not between lore and knowledge but rather between "disciplinary rigor" and "a complex problem [that] requires a complex solution" (128). This pairing does not leave the complex problem to go searching, hat in hand, for epistemological approval. Rather, it assumes that the facts produced by disciplinarity are not, in and of themselves, equipped to address what Harkin calls the "quotidian concerns" of classroom work (127). *Quotidian,* unfortunately, is saddled with connotations of the mundane and the banal (precisely the level at which Dewey wanted to do philosophic work). Harkin cites a growing list of thinkers, including Phelps, Freire, and Richard Ohmann, who have tried to intellectualize the quotidian, claiming "that acts of teaching do not merely disseminate knowledge but actually produce it" (124). Most important, lore opens a way past two occupational psychoses: recipe swapping on the one hand and scientism on the other. Echoing Berthoff, Harkin complains that practitioners "rarely attend to the theoretical implications of their practice, even if they do adopt, adapt, and apply theoretical articulations" (125). But a "stricter" mode of disciplinarity alone cannot correct this tendency. (*Rigor,* we should remember, is one half of the term *rigor mortis.*) "The irregular ad hoc procedures of lore are nondisciplinary, to be sure. But it seems possible to construe them also as postdisciplinary in their willingness to use, but refusal to be constrained by, existing conventions of knowledge production" (Harkin 130–31). The postdisciplinary is situated knowledge.

As with the kinetic taxonomies of casuistry, lore "arranges its data serially, spatially, paratactically, like a rhizome, however they work" (Harkin 134). Yet the kinetic development of taxonomies is not random. There is a logic to them, even if that logic cannot be expressed in either deductive or inductive terms. Nor is Harkin's endorsement of lore uncritical: "To recuperate lore is not simply to stop being disciplinary and start acting like a rhizome. Merely embracing lore would mean connecting events and explanations haphazardly" (134). Instead, lore is "a site and a moment at which differing *praxes meet as praxes*" (134; emphasis added). Like rhetoric, like casuistic stretching, lore is best practiced consciously and openly. In this "postdisciplinary" conversation,

> lore . . . elides without denying the opposition between theory and practice. And the informed intuition that produces that elision may, I would assert, be called theory—not in the sense of a meta-discourse, a generalized account of a practice to which all instances of that practice can be referred, but rather as a way of coping, contending with the overdetermined words of knowledge production. (134)

Dewey's word for this kind of work is *experience,* and I would suggest that practitioners adopt *experience* instead of *lore* as our quotidian keyword. Lore itself has perhaps become "overdetermined" or at least carries too much baggage to do any (post)disciplinary heavy lifting. I am thinking particularly here of Fulkerson's misreading of Harkin in "The Epistemic Paradoxes of 'Lore': From *The Making of Knowledge in Composition* to the Present (Almost)." Fulkerson simultaneously accuses Harkin of (a) playing the anti-foundationalist "card" that undermines knowledge as information and (b) insisting that Mina Shaughnessy's work is "just as strong a candidate for 'knowledge' as the most rigorous of quantitative findings" (59). Fulkerson is right to observe that one cannot at once deny the conventional idea of knowledge and then claim to offer something that meets that convention. But that reading of Harkin ignores the classroom context in which she places her argument. In the classroom, we produce a species of knowledge that seeks to solve particular problems. As with Atwill's rendering of *techne,* we are talking about knowledge that "is never a static, normative body of knowledge" and that "marks a domain of human intervention and invention" (7). This is why Harkin calls practitioner knowledge postdisciplinary. It has standards, even if they are not the standards of disciplinarity.

As Fulkerson describes, Harkin imagines a new kind of composition conference at which videotaped examples of teacher praxes would be discussed by a panel of theorists, "representatives of disciplinary ways of knowing, experienced in thinking through the implications of a practice. This conference would reverse the usual practice by which practitioners take from theorists ideas that they think will work" (Harkin 137). By starting with teacher experience, we would paradoxically avoid the temptation of the Monday Morning Question by making it the occasion, not the objection. Yet this conference would include "representatives of disciplinary ways of knowing." Contrary to Fulkerson's claims, Harkin does not reject the idea that there is a disciplinary knowledge as such; rather, she rejects the idea that the best classroom practice can be derived from such knowledge *and* that therefore best classroom practice should not count as a kind of knowledge. Harkin's idea is also thoroughly Deweyan insofar as it includes traditional content knowledge as part of the method of experience. We might, therefore, imagine a panel that would include Susan Jarratt as an expert on the sophists along with Fulkerson as an expert on modes of written argument. Unfortunately, Fulkerson mocks this idea: "As I revise this chapter in November of 2008, I can't help thinking of some CNN panel observing a speech of Sarah Palin or Barack Obama prior to offering their 'expert' commentary" ("Epistemic" 59). This remark shows a serious lack of faith in our own expertise, let alone in our ability to be rigorous and respectful. Fulkerson then insists, with some exasperation, that if we were to follow Harkin's procedure, "narrative claims would be 'settled' by a discussion of outside expert observers—a combination of authority, tradition, and consensus" (59). I am not sure that Harkin would say that sort of discussion would "settle" practitioner knowledge, since any experience produced in such a conference would subsequently have to be translated for new contexts. (Again, Fulkerson seems to be under the impression that a conference panel discussion could have the power to instantly become dogma.) More important, it seems odd, at least in a field that studies rhetoric, to reject the value of authority, tradition, and consensus—all of which are means of accessing other people's experience.

What Harkin is after, finally, is what she describes as "'an environmental-impact statement' for writing pedagogy" (126), a phrase that recalls the project of the present book: a way to identify and cultivate sustainable pedagogical experience. In effect, we are trying to answer the Tuesday Morning Question. Harkin's conference would obviate the usual challenge ("What am I supposed to do with all this theory when I pass through the classroom door?") since our central artifact is the classroom itself. Instead, our main questions would focus on what we are to do with a particular experience of student writing: "How do I make a sustainable resource of that experience, particularly an experience that, in a compelling way, fails to meet expectations?" Given a choice between the imaginative and the bureaucratic, there is no doubt that we should err on the side of the imaginative. As Burke writes in *Counter-Statement,* "We may depend upon it that even a world rigorously schooled in doubt will be dogmatical enough" (113). But that choice is ultimately false, and the real challenge is to bureaucratize pedagogical doubt. Harkin's approach is sustainable insofar as it makes such doubt absolute and constant. Most important, it offers a blueprint for a casuistic inquiry into the work of composition. We start with a case, a particular experience, and try to understand that case through previous experience. We avoid a deductive result by simultaneously demanding that we retrofit our previous experience to be "compatible" with the present experience. Indeed, the only problem with Harkin's proposal is not that it appeals to authority, tradition, and consensus but that it does not make that appeal—its potential benefits, its potential problems—explicit enough.

Since I cannot produce this kind of conference in these pages, I want to close by producing the kind of pedagogical casuistic analysis for which I have been arguing. For my artifact, I turn to a piece that appeared in *College Composition and Communication*'s "Staffroom Interchange," a section that offered brief descriptions of pedagogical applications. One might just as easily have turned to the Exercise Exchange, which Berthoff wanted closed down until there was a matching theory exchange (*Making* 33). The Staffroom Interchange was a regular feature in *CCC* until 1992, when editor Richard Gebhardt dropped it from the journal's pages for reasons that will recall North's mixed feelings about lore: "The title of the section—suggesting, many people have grumbled over the years, brief notes tacked on the coffee room bulletin board—remained a problem, especially since the section had evolved to include 'fuller essays of application, speculation, and introspection,' as well as the short, classroom pieces it long had carried" (9–10). North might worry about this development, which would purportedly confuse the product of such inquiry. But from a Deweyan perspective, the Staffroom Interchange seems to suffer from the same problem to which Berthoff points: a lack of theoretical or philosophical formation. The case-based, kinetically taxonomic workings of casuistry allow us to form our experience philosophically; by making such practice absolute and constant, we can avoid the confusion about which North worries.

I take as my example a piece published in 1970 by Grace McLaughlin, and I choose it entirely for its title: "An Experiment in Translating Experience into Abstraction." All the keywords are here: *experiment, experience,* and even *abstraction.* Though I have not used this term often in the preceding pages, abstraction is at the center of the argument insofar as we are asking whether present experience can be translated through abstraction into a resource for future experience. In addition to the keywords, we find in McLaughlin's piece a sort of proleptic ecology for the arguments that would concern composition over the next three decades: questions about expressivism and social construction, personal writing and academic discourse communities, process and excess. The lesson is an experiment in invention in which students are paired off. One is blindfolded, and the other leads the student throughout the classroom building without ever using language: "The guide was to firmly hold the hand or elbow of his blindfolded partner at all times" (270). During the next meeting, the students reflected on their experience in "a good discussion" during which "everyone had something to say" (271). This strange pedagogy exhibits expressive, almost happening-like elements, but the design also has a social aspect. Not only are students dependent on their fellows, but the results of their experience are first articulated in discussion. Most important for the present discussion, it is difficult to imagine how we might assess such a pedagogy without Jarratt's black-market economy.

Though she does not invoke Dewey, McLaughlin puts the idea behind her experiment in Deweyan language: "By 'translating experience into abstractions,' I mean struggling with an idea, *thinking through a problem in terms of what one does know through experience*" (269; emphasis added). This is the classic Deweyan situation of relating the new and the given, and from it, we might construct a maxim: *Students think through problems in terms of* their *experience, not ours.* This emphasis helps McLaughlin avoid a problem vividly described by Richard Ohmann: Too often, composition imagines a writer who is "without social origins and without needs that would spring from his origins. He has no history. Hence the writing he does and the skills he acquires are detached from those parts of himself not encompassed by his new identity as a *student*" (148). Shall our students shed *their experience* (words I use here instead of *themselves*) at the door of our classrooms? Following Dewey, by the spirit if not the letter, McLaughlin insists that pedagogy cannot force students to make such a choice. We might detect another pedagogical maxim: *Be wary of occasion design that separates the student from his or her own history.* At Harkin's conference, one of the respondents, having watched a film of McLaughlin's class, might offer this maxim. "How," I can hear Harkin or Berthoff asking, "does this lesson draw on the student's prior experience toward his or her new invention? Where is the connection?" The lack of connection would not, of course, mean that the lesson was a failure, but it might mean that future versions of this lesson would have to imagine an answer to that Ohmannian question.

McLaughlin urges her readers to consider that we frequently require students to divide themselves. "What we inadvertently do is to elevate him out of the realm of his relevant experience" (270). Once again, we see the beginnings of casuistry in that McLaughlin adopts what Berthoff would later articulate in the basic maxim: *Begin with where they are.* McLaughlin, however, offers a more powerful articulation of this maxim: *Do not elevate students out of their own experience.* This does not mean that we don't "challenge" (i.e., offer new experience to) our students. "The problem then is how to make the life experience—the conscious development of ideas which people care about—into a classroom experience" (270). Thus McLaughlin's experiment, in which she invites students to get in touch with experience in its most basic form.

McLaughlin's rationale for her lesson anticipates the question of method that would eventually animate the field's anxieties about process. "Clearly some students do learn to use the methods we have so neatly provided for them, but rather than enhancing the thinking process these methods become a substitute for thinking" (270). She also worries that the "presentation of a method of development (analogy, definition, etc.) gives the student an easy out, a formula in which he merely fills in the blanks" (270). McLaughlin does not speak in the terms we would later use, and it would be the task of pedagogical casuistry to make those connections more explicit. At the time of McLaughlin's actual lesson, casuists might have made connections to the expressivism emerging, or to the romanticism that preceded it (as historians later would). The purpose of such connections would not be to enforce theoretical purity but rather to understand the particularity of the lesson at hand. The ways in which a lesson fails to conform to a theory are just as important as the ways in which it does conform.

In addition, such connections would allow us to speculate about evaluation. When the students write about the assignment, McLaughlin notices improvement in their writing, including "success in grasping and developing ideas" (271). Here is where we run into the deficiencies of lore—namely, claims that cannot be contested in any sustained way. We would need to see written evidence that the students had grasped and developed ideas, though this evidence would have to be argued for, given that there are no settled criteria for such claims. (Perhaps we could compose a sort of negative maxim: *Never make claims about student experience without evidence that they themselves have produced.*) Without these connections, we would have to rely entirely on a black-market economy. By Jarratt's own description, this would be impossible since everyone in the class already knows about the assignment. McLaughlin seems to suggest just such an economy, writing that the students displayed "an honest spontaneity toward the assignment" (271).

Of course, we should welcome honest spontaneity, even if it is hard to imagine a group of people acting spontaneously all at once. The language of "excess" breaks down, since everything cannot be an excess.

In addition, McLaughlin would have to articulate some relationship between this experiment and previous experiments. That is, she would have to begin to construct a taxonomy or would have to link her experiment to some other, incipient taxonomy. The problem with these pedagogical narratives is not that they are so compelling that they distort or distract from reality (as North seems to think). The problem is that without a taxonomy, or a network reshaping our interpretations of the present and the past, there is no way to put narrative claims under scrutiny. North and Fulkerson are not wrong to worry that lore affords no means of scrutiny. But a taxonomic casuistry can allow us to think about those claims while maintaining some fidelity to the situations from which they sprung. In a longer piece, McLaughlin might describe the experiments performed by other teachers that have inspired her classroom intervention. This description would not necessarily be a replication in the sense that we usually associate with scientific experimentation, but we could at least describe the intellectual heritage on which we draw. Taxonomic articulation would offer the meeting place for praxes so that McLaughlin's readers would have a sense of how to adapt her lesson before adopting it. This kind of pedagogical casuistry would not finally produce knowledge but would collect experiences and gather praxes. The teacher about whom North worries—the teacher whose visionary inspiration is about to take a beating from the who-shows-up—would have something much better than a set of theories. He would have instead a set of experiences whose particularity would automatically demand rearticulation for a new context. The adhoccery of such experiences would maintain the suppleness of the inspiration. Later, practitioners producing new pedagogies would refer us to McLaughlin, whose lesson would have become part of a new kinetic assembly of experiences.

The reader might reasonably ask whether I am suggesting that composition follow the practice of historical casuistry and produce elaborate and immense volumes of pedagogical case studies. Why not? The kind of discipline, or postdiscipline, imagined by post-pedagogy has to include fora that offer something other than the usual classroom journal article. Certainly, the baroque complexity of casuistry seems unwieldy and untenable in a culture driven by efficiency. But the complexity of casuistry is precisely what recommends it. As Richard B. Miller notes in *Casuistry and Modern Ethics*, "Collective deliberation is notoriously inefficient, requiring time to gather information and to organize forums for debating facts, interests, and practical needs" (11). Deliberation, according to Burke, occasions "organized distrust, 'protest made easy,' a babble of discordant voices, a colossal getting in one's own way" (*CS* 114). Pedagogically speaking, composition needs to be able to get in its own way, and a casuistic conversation would allow us to preach and practice the gospel of inefficiency. Too often, our pedagogical narratives proclaim our efficiency, as John Schilb writes in his final editor's column in *College English*. Writing about teaching, he observes, offers a mixture of

> ethnography with aspects of literature. Much can be said for this approach. But it leaves those of us who write about pedagogy with a composing problem of our own. How can we now gain readers' trust? If, as so many of us do, we eschew a rhetoric of science or use it cautiously, what means of building credibility remain? This challenge is especially great when we describe our personal classroom performance. Readers may think we're out to hide its flaws. . . . To head off suspicions that the story is just too rosy to be true, a good move is to mention at least some uncertainties, dilemmas, stumbles. Further, when writers tout their classroom habits—*instructional methods that have served multiple courses*—they gain credibility if they concede that these measures haven't been foolproof. I'm skeptical when I see teaching achievements described in present tense: for example, "Through this exercise, my students hatch good theses." The implication is that the author's classes always go according to plan. But hardly ever can pedagogy be smoothly ritualistic; in any classroom, the unexpected can loom. (514–15; emphasis added)

Obviously, we can add Schilb's to the voices (North; Fulkerson, "Epistemic") worried that our pedagogical conversation is insufficiently rigorous. For me, however, the most important moment of this passage concerns those times when we discuss "instructional methods that have served multiple courses." Here, when we are speaking of portability, the danger of the triumphalist narrative is most acute. "It worked last semester and the semester before that," we are tempted to think, "so I can run it again without revision." At the same time, a lesson or unit that has played out in multiple courses makes the possibility of casuistic deliberation most available. Why did case A seem to succeed and case B didn't?

Following Schilb's observations, we might compose another maxim for pedagogical casuistry: *A lesson should never work three times.* We might also begin our casuistic deliberation with a counterintuitive taxonomy: "Lessons That Blew Up in Our Faces." (It might take some courage to publish a case for such a taxonomy, but once started, its coral growth would be limitless.) However we proceed, "change will be wrought in the journals and forums devoted to discussions of writing" (Rickert, *Acts* 197). I am not suggesting that *CCC* or *College English* appoint a high casuist to the editorial board (though it would look fantastic on a vita), but I am suggesting that our electronic journals, where digital writing would allow the revision necessary for kinetic taxonomies, might feature casuistic versions of the Exercise Exchange or the old Staffroom Interchange. Teachers would post case studies, and users would offer analysis, whether that be an articulation of maxims, a description of taxonomies, or a rearrangement of taxonomy. Such pedagogical crowdsourcing would help us resist the temptation to rigidity or rule making as new voices would continue to oxygenate our developing networks and ecologies. At this point in our disciplinary history, we could rely on a torrent of criticism if our imaginative did become too bureaucratized. Berthoff's Caveat, now capitalized as a fundamental maxim, would be posted in a sidebar: "NCTE would not be allowed to operate [the Exercise Exchange] unless they instituted a Theory Exchange. And you couldn't get a recipe unless you also went there" (*Making* 33). In fact, the interface could be arranged so that no one could post a case study without also posting a theory or a story of uncertainty. For it is there—in uncertainty—that we are most likely to capture, and to intellectualize, our pedagogical practice.

I realize that what I am imagining here seems to be a contradiction in terms: a redesigned House of Lore. The whole point of North's metaphor is that the House is not susceptible to design. That wildness seems inviting when the alternative is a House of Law, cold, dusty, and dank. By contrast, the House of Lore is full of mysteries and surprises. Like some postmodern Hogwarts, the staircases move, the walls shudder, the ceilings buckle, the floors give way. But its jerry-rigged construction can also make for exhausting living. Yes, the system that law imposes may frustrate; equally frustrating, however, is lore's haphazard and half-hearted chase after a system that it does not really want to reach. One imagines wings that lead nowhere, exposed wires dangling from ceilings, pipes dripping water onto unfinished floors. This is why the House of Lore seems unsustainable as a disciplinary home.

What I have tried to imagine instead is a "House of Pedagogical Casuistry." Admittedly, this phrase is unlikely to catch on in the disciplinary patois. The same is probably true for the "Reef of Experience Accretion" and the "Taxonomic Parlor of Maxim Manufacture." (The "House of Lore," like the activity it seeks to dismiss, is simply too catchy to die a natural death.) But as ugly as my alternatives are, they at least suggest the complexity of trying to intellectualize the uncertainty of teaching. The question is how we bring rigor to the expression and experience of contingency. In a sense, the conversation I have imagined is one in which teachers attempt to articulate practical wisdom, to imaginatively bureaucratize. I think that such a blend of *techne* and praxis is possible, but it is not necessarily natural, as Aristotle's original distinction between art and action suggests. Nor does it seem intuitive to enunciate experience in Dewey's strange way, as a word meaning both data and method at the very same moment. The habit of thought

that opposes a House of Lore to a House of Law is not easily discarded. Nor can (or should) compositionists look at pedagogy free
of the arguments offered by those who would move us past pedagogy. There is, as they suggest, no absolute naïveté available. But
as Dewey suggests, there is a "cultivated naïveté" available, though
it "can be acquired only through the discipline of severe thought"
(*EN* 37–38). This is the challenge of pedagogical work: to practice
what Zen masters call "beginner's mind," the intentional habit of
having a fresh attitude. Cultivated naïveté, beginner's mind, undis-
ciplined expertise, all leading to a kind of pedagogical *sprezzatura*.
The discipline that would encourage these habits would have to
be severe. Ironically, given its moral reputation for laxity, casuistry
offers such discipline. A pedagogical casuistry would require not
simply a dialectic between theory and practice, or the universal and
the particular, but rather new articulations of a familiar activity,
leading to a discipline—or, as Dewey might suggest, a culture—of
pedagogical experience.

NOTES

Prologue: The Tuesday Morning Question

1. Phelps insists on this same caveat: "Teaching involves activity with practical-moral consequences for others, so that it is not only formed on the model of phronesis (in being hermeneutical), but actually *is* phronesis in the original sense of conduct subject to regulative ideas of right and good" (217). Certainly pedagogy requires interpretive skill, but it is not coequal to interpretive skill.

2. Whereas Aristotle's *phronesis* still involves a dialectic between the universal and the particular, or the practical and the theoretical, Dewey's experience attempts to avoid this sort of dialectic, which Dewey would call a form of analysis but not an actual feature of experience. The universal and the particular can be separated through analysis; in experience, Dewey insists, they are inextricable. The same is true, of course, of the theory–practice binary. What makes this distinction corrosive is the idea that it is a distinction at all. Teachers always operate with theory, even if the theory is invisible to them, and theory itself constitutes a form of practice insofar as it changes or challenges habits of thought. Moreover, though I have invoked Sánchez and second his objection to the essentialism he finds in hermeneutics, in fairness I should note that he would likely reject my nomination of experience as a more productive description of the art of teaching. Sánchez's purpose is to insist that composition focus its attention on *writing*, not the meaning that writing either creates or communicates. He is not interested in the idea, concept, or experience that writing might be said to capture (94). Whether he would say the same about pedagogy, or whether he would object to the way I have casuistically stretched his argument, I don't know. I would say, however, that Dewey's ideas of experience and communication are so deeply intertwined that he, too, would be troubled by the idea that one "uses" language to communicate

experience. For Dewey, communication *is* an experience, and experience a communication. I discuss this more fully in Chapter 3.

1. Inspired Adhoccery

1. As we see in Chapter 2, the question of pedagogy may involve "a setting aside of Virgil's *Aeneid* and an accepting of Ovid's *Metamorphoses*" (Vitanza, *Negation* 61). Virgil's hero does finally end his wanderings and manages to found a city and an empire. Ovid's heroes and heroines are too busy floating around.

2. Certainly, Haynes's vision of the field could be contested. Almost all the pedagogical groundings she cites—grammar, style, aims, modes, claims, grounds, and warrants—have been seriously challenged in our scholarship, though perhaps these linger too long in our teaching and our textbooks.

3. I do not mean to suggest here that Quintilian and Haynes come to the same conclusion. Far from it. For more on this, see Richard Lanham's "The Q Question" in *The Electronic Word*.

4. Not all postpedagogues refuse to speak of teaching. While Dobrin seems resolute in rejecting a pedagogical conversation, most postprocess thinkers are ultimately arguing about what goes on in the classroom. The third sophistic school, meanwhile, is explicitly interested in the classroom, as evidenced by many of the writers I address in Chapter 2.

5. I imagine many readers will assume that Alasdair MacIntyre's *After Virtue* is the inspiration for my title. Though I am familiar with that book, the similarity did not occur to me until long after I had settled on *After Pedagogy*. The same is true for Terry Eagleton's *After Theory* and Stephen Yarborough's *After Rhetoric*. For some reason, I came upon these "after" titles after I had settled on my own. (Invention, postpedagogues might here observe, works in mysterious ways.) However else the title has been used, I do not mean to suggest either (a) that we can really break away from pedagogy or (b) that we could or should "return" to some "simpler time."

6. This proverb is quoted far and wide to suggest the uncertain nature of practice and the fleeting nature of experience. In her *Democratic Paradox*, for example, Chantal Mouffe invokes Machado to inform her explication of liberal democracy, a combination that she insists will remain a sterile oxymoron unless it is rearticulated into a generative paradox: "There is no necessary relation between those two distinct traditions but only a contingent historical articulation" (3).

In any modern democracy, we face "the modern impossibility of providing a final guarantee, a definite legitimation" (2). Paulo Freire invokes the poem to similar purpose in *We Make the Road by Walking*, a discussion of radical education between Freire and his fellow educator Myles Horton. Just as they make the book by talking it, Freire and Horton make the road of educational reform by walking it and coauthor the book by speaking it.

2. Is Teaching Still Impossible?

1. My procedure will be to divide the discussion into the postprocess and sophistic camps I described earlier. This division is somewhat artificial. There are obvious overlaps in theoretical resources, practical intention, and even dramatis personae; these overlaps undermine any hard-and-fast distinction or even a claim of twin "schools." The recent (2011) collection *Beyond Postprocess* (Dobrin, Rice, and Vastola), for example, features writers who might be labeled "postprocess" and writers who might be labeled "third sophistic." Yet there does seem to be a difference in attitude toward pedagogy. Postprocess thinkers make greater efforts to avoid pedagogical discussion. Though Kent and Olson seem more comfortable with composition's pedagogical activity than Dobrin does, they seem to prefer ignoring pedagogy to attacking it. While the third sophistic thinkers share postprocess's skepticism of systems and procedures, they seem more confident about the idea of pedagogy, or at least the activity of teaching, as being central in composition. Still, these differences are not fundamentally important, and my distinction is largely designed to maintain some fidelity to the original scholarly networks from which and within which these arguments emerged.

2. For more on this debate, see Breuch; Fulkerson ("Of Pre- and Post-Process"); Matsuda; and McComiskey.

3. In "The Great Paradigm Shift and Its Legacy for the Twenty-First Century," Lynn Bloom recounts a job interview she had during the height of process: "'What's the magic word?' asked my interviewer in 1977, looking for a codirector of a National Writing Project affiliate. 'Process,' I shot back" (32). Needless to say, Bloom was hired on the spot. Barbara Couture writes of hearing from public school teachers "that they knew all about the writing process: I learned from them that on Monday morning in each of their classes, their students must do 'prewriting'; on Wednesday they must 'draft' their papers; and on Friday, without fail, they must 'revise' them"

(30). As she observes, "Pedantry is clearly one paradigm the process movement had failed to subvert" (30). David Russell writes of a similar experience; he recalls seeing the writing process captured by a few stark posters: "Each of the posters—obviously commercially produced—contained in large black type one word. PREWRITE. WRITE. REVISE. EDIT" ("Activity" 80). When I taught middle school, I had similar posters in my classroom. I have to admit that I was glad I had them. As an inexperienced teacher, I found it helpful to be reminded that writers needed time to rewrite and revise.

4. To preview the argument of the next chapter a bit: Dewey, whose theory supports much of the argument of this book, might suggest that Kent is still begging the question of how communication happens. Kent too widely separates the communicator from the context of communication. More on this in Chapter 3.

5. Dobrin's *Postcomposition* also suggests that postpedagogy—which we might call a descendant of postprocess—offers a welcome "pedagogical violence," which "is not to be read as a new way of teaching students how to write [n]or in any literal classroom understanding of pedagogy" (190). To be fair, however, Dobrin, Rice, and Vastola insist that they are "not opposed to composition studies' pedagogical imperative, but more interested in questions and theories of writing not trapped by disciplinary expectations of the pedagogical" (14).

6. Kent rejects Fish's stance as an "implicit Cartesianism" and argues that "Fish possesses no convincing response to the skeptic or to those who charge him with relativism" (*Paralogic* 79–80). If we can know things *only* through interpretive communities, as Fish seems to suggest, then his position "advocates a brand of radical subjectivism that denies our ability to know anything outside the interpretive community in which we find ourselves" (*Paralogic* 79). Against this position, Kent offers Donald Davidson's notion of "prior theories," the theories a given listener brings to a given utterance, and "passing theories," the theories a listener actually ends up using to interpret a given utterance (*Paralogic* 86–87). Shuttling back and forth between prior and passing theories, listeners are able to make "highly accurate guesses" about what others are trying to communicate (*Paralogic* 86). Whatever their conceptual differences, Kent and Fish share a radical skepticism toward the possibility of theorized teaching, with Fish rejecting the theory and Kent the teaching.

7. As Chapter 4 suggests, these bromides may be more productively referred to as "maxims," rules of thumb that guide thought rather

than deductively applying principles or theories. Maxims might also be a more useful replacement for the idea of passing theories.

8. Even Petraglia, so sure of composition's uselessness as a subject, is also sure that we can teach situations. While he is skeptical of our ability to teach rhetorical production, he is confident that we can teach hermeneutic interpretation (62). The purpose of the WAC courses he envisions "would not be to improve students' writing skills but to make students informed consumers of writing discourse *in the hope that they may become better producers of it as well*" (63; emphasis added). Petraglia here seems to say that we should teach what we can teach in the hope that it trickles down to what we want to teach. But why should we be confident that we can teach interpretation any better than we can teach invention? And why should we be confident that teaching interpretation will teach invention?

9. Vitanza credits Susan Jarratt with naming a group of nineteenth- and twentieth-century rhetoricians (including Nietzsche, Heidegger, Derrida, Feyerabend, Deleuze, Lyotard, Rorty) as the "third sophistic" ("Critical" 45, "'Some More'" 134, n1).

10. Which is not to suggest that Rickert endorses the cultural studies project. Certainly it seems that he is sympathetic to the content of the project's politics, but his book does not represent an alternative attempt to achieve cultural studies' outcomes.

11. In her essay "Negation and the Contradictory Technics of Rhetoric," Kelly Pender suggests that our anxieties about our own power and student resistance might not matter. She argues that the division between the instrumentality (usefulness) and materiality (exuberance) of language is false, since any language use is too indeterminate to be so labeled. She goes on to observe this problem in Davis's *Breaking Up*, where Davis says first that exuberance can be suppressed and then insists that exuberance can never be suppressed (14, n14). These somewhat conflicting ideas also manifest themselves in Rickert's argument, where Acts are seen as both inevitable and intentional.

12. Again, the third sophistic school attempts to avoid the trap of dialectic: "To be sub/versive of the Law is still at once to be 'subject' to the Law" (Vitanza, "Concerning" 397).

13. If rule-governed procedures snuff out the spirit, vitalism, argues Young, is nothing but spirit: "The new romanticism presents the teacher of composition with a difficult problem, i.e., how does one teach a mystery?" (55). This possibility seems to Young as untenable

as those methods that set down "a finite series of steps that can be carried out consciously and mechanically . . . and if properly carried out always yields a correct result" (57). Mystery to the left of him and geometry to the right, Young turns to heuristics, the method of the "new classicists," as he calls them and among whom he counts himself. Heuristics are offered to counter what Young sees as a problematic binary of the "expository mode" on one side and the "hypothetical mode" on the other (55).

3. The Cultivation of Naïveté

1. This vision of *techne* seems to echo Eric Charles White's idea of *kaironomia. Kairos,* argues White, cannot be understood or appreciated apart from *nomos,* which might be defined as the customs or traditions produced by a community. *Kairos* may indeed be "unprecedented, as a moment of decision, a moment of crisis"; it is "impossible, therefore, to intervene successfully in the course of events merely on the basis of past experience" (14). Tradition alone, he goes on to argue, is insufficient for addressing unanticipated contingency. White, therefore, appears to endorse a Gorgian rather than Aristotelian view of invention. Yet White also tempers this view by acknowledging that *kairos* cannot operate entirely outside tradition without risking "incomprehensibility if not incoherence" (41). Gorgias, a sophist and White's test case for the power of *kairos,* must finally articulate the discoveries of *kairos* in a context shaped, at least in part, by *nomos:* "The desire that thought should continually innovate . . . is accompanied by the recognition that thinking must become complicit with tradition if it would communicate with an audience" (41). Innovation that challenges tradition also comes from within that tradition. "Didactic and speculative impulses," White writes, "endlessly revise and correct one another" (152). Rhetoric and composition's reexamination of *techne* and *tuche* could be plotted along similar lines.

2. Yet long before even Quintilian, both navigation and rhetoric were seen as *techne,* productive arts that offered "a domain of human intervention and invention" (Atwill 7). As Janet Atwill makes clear throughout *Rhetoric Reclaimed,* "The art of the helmsman can only be exercised within the framework of the uncertainty and instability of the sea. The play of the tiller cannot be dissociated from the waves" (Marcel Deitenne and Jean-Pierre Vernant, qtd. in Atwill 95). The same could be said for the *dynamis* of rhetoric, which also cannot be separated from the contingency in which it operates.

Though Atwill suggests that Quintilian tried to maintain this association between navigation and rhetoric in his *Institutes, techne* eventually came to be equated with the handbook tradition of firm rules designed to stave off uncertainty (6).

3. In some ways, *experience* is the wrong word to use. Dewey would later wish that he had used *culture* rather than *experience* because experience simply carried too much intellectual baggage. I have stuck with *experience,* however, simply because it is is the term that Dewey actually used. Moreover, I think *experience* captures something important for the present discussion—namely, that new situations are always the products, if only in part, of previous situations. That is not to say that *culture* could not do similar work, and occasionally I use the terms interchangeably in this chapter.

4. I'll be using the following abbreviations for Dewey's works in this chapter:

   AE = *Art as Experience* (1934)
   DE = *Democracy and Education* (1916)
   EE = *Experience and Education* (1938)
   EN = *Experience and Nature* (1925)
   HWT = *How We Think* (1910)
   KK = *Knowing and the Known* (1949)
   LSA = *Liberalism and Social Action* (1935)
   QC = *The Quest for Certainty* (1929)
   SS = *The School and Society* (1900)

   A note on my use of *Experience and Nature*: The Dover edition I used, originally published in 1958, is a reproduction of the second edition of the book. The book's initial publication date is 1925; the second edition was published in 1929. (A second impression of the 1925 edition, appearing in 1926, both corrected old errors and introduced new ones.) In addition to many small typographical changes, the 1929 edition features a substantially revised first chapter. In 1948, Dewey set about revising the book again, but he did not complete it before he died in 1952. The quotations I have relied on from the Dover edition of *Experience and Nature* match the edition produced in the Southern Illinois University Press (SIUP) edition of Dewey's collected works. Though I have not used the SIUP collection exclusively, I describe my use of *Experience and Nature* because it is so central to my argument.

5. Curiously, however, she supports this claim by citing not a compositionist but rather Louise Rosenblatt, whom Emig describes as "our closest intellectual ally in literature research" (150). It is interesting

to note that the earliest disciplinary claim for Dewey is premised on the work of someone whom the claimant considers outside our field. Emig's reference to Rosenblatt came at a time when the term *compositionist* may not have been as conventional as it is today. Yet it is obvious from Emig's use of *ally* that she sees herself moving between distinct scholarly communities. My intention in making these observations is of course not to police the borders of our field but rather to suggest that our Deweyan "tradition" may not always have been as thoroughly ours.

6. Ultimately, I resist Russell's conclusion because it ends up casting writing as "merely" a means of communication; in other words, it depends on the very sort of dualism it claims to reject. Moreover, Russell's argument assumes that Dewey's idea of content and our idea of disciplinarity are the same things. Dewey, however, imagined the content supporting a more democratic mode of living rather than the specialization called for in disciplinarity.

7. In fact, Dewey speaks of emergence in ways that prefigure contemporary complexity theory: "The transactional view of emergence . . . will not expect merely to report the advent out of the womb of nature of something that still retains an old non-natural independence and isolation. . . . It will seek enriched descriptions of primary life processes in their environments and of the more complex behavioral processes in theirs" (*KK* 129).

8. Unfortunately, Kent's reading of Dewey (like Russell's) is somewhat cursory, relying exclusively on *Experience and Nature*. This brief foray leads Kent to make assertions about Dewey that are only half-true. Kent writes that Dewey adopts a resolutely instrumental view of language: "The character of language—if language can be said to possess such a thing—may be described only through an account of language's instrumental social uses" (*Paralogic* 10). Yet Dewey actually sees language as both instrumental *and* consummatory, as possessing both pragmatic and aesthetic qualities. Language does work in the world—an understanding that Dewey certainly maintains—but it also can be appreciated *as* language.

9. See also Crick's *Democracy and Rhetoric: John Dewey on the Arts of Becoming*. As a recovering Hegelian, Dewey was skeptical of the dualism that underwrites dialectic. Regarding the tension between experience and nature, Dewey writes that dialectic is incapable of bridging the gulf that has grown between the two terms because of their conventional meanings (*EN* 1a–2a). On Dewey's early Hegelianism, see Chapters 1–4 of Westbrook.

10. Dewey's attitude toward "logic" certainly suggests the rhetorical cast of his thought. Dewey objects to the "supernatural" view of logic that is "supposed to have its basis in what is beyond human conduct and relationships" (*EN* 169).

11. In *The School and Society*, Dewey describes language as one of the four basic impulses of education. The other three impulses are inquiry, making, and art, and these, too, have a rhetorical flavor. To students of Aristotle, the rhetorical tendencies of making and art will be apparent: "The instinct of investigation seems to grow out of the combination of the constructive impulse with the conversational" (44). Inquiry—another term for Dewey's notion of empiricism—is communal insofar as communication is the medium through which our experiences become meaningful.

12. See Bitzer; Vatz; Consigny; Biesecker ("Rethinking"); and Edbauer.

13. Perhaps *scheme* can be read with a sophistic tone. Consider this passage from *How We Think*: "It is significant that many words for intelligence suggest the idea of a circuitous, evasive activity—often with a sort of intimation of even moral obliquity. The bluff, hearty man goes straight (and stupidly, it is implied) at some work. The intelligent man is cunning, shrewd (crooked), wily, subtle, crafty, artful, designing—the idea of indirection is involved" (110).

14. We might recall Raúl Sánchez's insistence that "pedagogy should be theorized not as an important component of culture (though it certainly is that) but as culture itself—culture as an aggregate of quasi-autonomous teaching and learning relationships" ("First" 192). Sánchez's touchstone is Gramsci, but it could just as easily be Dewey, for whom experience was another name for culture (Menand 427). Sánchez adds, "Pedagogy is not only the explicit act of imparting lessons in an authorized educational setting; it is also, and more importantly, the production and transmission of values at various levels and locations of a given society. From a variety of sources, one learns—generally and specifically—how to be part of a larger group" ("First" 192). This is a perfect summation of the aspiration of the Deweyan educational project.

15. We might note, by the way, that the verb is *to renew*, not *to new*. Dewey would certainly agree that we need not be bound by the structures of conventional language. But it is worth considering that our usual verb for making something new is to *renew* it, to make it new *again*, suggesting the basic idea behind Dewey's concept of experience: we make what is new out of what is old.

4. Unprincipled Pedagogy

1. For Burke's work in this chapter, I use the common abbreviations:
   ATH = Attitudes toward History (1937)
   CS = Counter-Statement (1931)
   GM = A Grammar of Motives (1945)

2. Informal casuistry endures, of course. "It takes place daily as persons ruminate about how they ought to act or argue about how others should act or have acted. It rings through the literature of our culture, from Homeric epic to *Schindler's List*. It takes up pages of newsprint and hours of television time. This activity consists of thinking and talking about how the circumstances of this or that case of moral perplexity fit the general norms, rules, standards, and principles of morality. This is casuistry in life" (Jonsen, "Casuistry: An Alternative?" 237).

3. For more on casuistry in rhetoric and composition, see McKee and Porter, Toner, and Wright.

4. This late dialogue was not the first time that Booth had urged English teachers to consider how casuistry might inform their teaching. He made a similar call in a 1998 essay titled "The Ethics of Teaching Literature." Borrowing his notion of the ethical from Alasdair MacIntyre, Booth argued that our understanding of ethical criticism should "shift us from judgments about specific commandments or codes toward . . . concern for the construction of a certain kind of person. Ethical thinking at its best has always pursued not literal 'thou shalt nots' but a range of 'virtues,' characteristic habits of behavior considered admirable" (42). To teach these sorts of habits, Booth encouraged casuistry. Practice in case-based reasoning would cultivate the kind of person who would not need to depend exclusively on rules in order to make sound ethical judgments. The importance of literature, he suggested, is that it "teaches effective casuistry: the counterbalancing of 'cases.' It is in stories that we learn to think about the 'virtual' cases that echo the cases we will meet when we return to the more disorderly, 'actual' world" (48). For Booth, casuistry is the means to the end of practical wisdom. For my purposes, casuistry is the means to a self-challenging method of pedagogical reflection and reinvention.

5. The literature on casuistry in medical ethics is enormous. Jonsen and Toulmin provide a good start, as does the work of Baruch Brody (*Life, Taking Issue*). See also Arras ("Getting"); Goodrich; Jonsen ("Casuistry," "Of Balloons," "Casuistry: An Alternative"); Kopleman; Peach; Strong; Tomlinson; and Toulmin ("National"). For

a good introduction to casuistry, see Jonsen's appropriately titled "Platonic Insults: Casuistical" and James Tallmon's entry on casuistry in the *Encyclopedia of Rhetoric*. See also Bedau; Kirk; and Richard B. Miller.

6. I am trying not to stretch the historical roots of casuistry too far. "As an explicit procedure for resolving moral problems," write Jonsen and Toulmin, "casuistry did not originate until after A.D. 1000" (101). My point here is not to make the anachronistic claim that Aristotle is a casuist. At times, he seems suspicious of particulars. In the *Rhetoric*, for example, he writes, "The art of medicine does not specify what is healthful for Socrates or Callias but for persons of a certain sort (this is a matter of art, while particulars are limitless and not knowable)—neither does rhetoric theorize about each opinion—what may seem so to Socrates or Hippias—but about what seems true to people of a certain sort, as is also true with dialectic" (1356b). He adds, "It is highly appropriate for well-enacted laws to define everything as exactly as possible and for as little as possible to be left to the judges" (1354a). This sentiment is not necessarily opposed to casuistry, since casuists can also work within a framework of well-enacted laws, but it does suggest a sensibility prominent in our own culture—namely, the sentiment that preset rules should be able to account for any particular that might later emerge.

7. For a contemporary treatment of this question, see the first chapter of Sandel's *Justice*.

8. For more on the Jesuits and casuistry, see Maryks.

9. This seems to run counter to Lyotard's claim that "one is without criteria, yet one must decide" (Lyotard and Thébaud 17). Where Dewey and Lyotard might agree is that the situation of justice, or morality, presents problems that cannot be decided by the criteria, or values, we possess as they are currently articulated.

10. Schwartz and Sharpe also describe the kind of black-market situation imagined by Jarratt: "Suppose you are grading term papers. You read one written by a student who is struggling to get a C in your course. It is decently written and coherently organized, and it has no major misunderstandings of key concepts. It is a B- paper, but it is by far the best work this student has done in your course. Next, you turn to one written by the smartest student in the class, someone who is effortlessly 'acing' everything you throw her way. It is well written and clearly organized, and it demonstrates fine comprehension. A solid B+, perhaps even an A-. But it lacks spark. It is not very original. It does not go very far beyond what was said

in class. This student could definitely have done a much better piece of work" ("Practical Wisdom" 377).

11. The Church originally defined usury as lending at *any* interest, and it had forbidden the practice on the grounds that it permitted such profit. Loans were permissible for those in need and only if no interest were charged. As economies changed, however, the perception (and construction) of usury began to change. The concept of "partnership" helped draw the distinction: "The crucial moral difference . . . rested on the sharing of risk. By introducing the concept of risk as a modality in the argument, the first step toward revision of the paradigm was taken" (Jonsen and Toulmin 185). Thus, the old principle of labor was stretched to include the new principle of risk.

12. Burke does not endorse casuistry unreservedly. In *A Rhetoric of Motives*, for example, he derides casuistry as the "Jesuit trick" (157).

13. For more on casuistry's role in law, see Sunstein and Levi.

14. This revival of casuistry, of course, did not persuade everyone. Casuistry's main detractors in medical ethics have argued that medieval and Renaissance casuistry developed against a background of widespread moral consensus. Today, however, we live in a pluralistic society: "We are Platonic perfectionists in saluting gold medallists in the Olympics, utilitarians in applying the principle of triage to the wounded in war, Lockeans in affirming rights over property; Christians in idealizing charity, compassion, and equal moral worth; and followers of Kant and Mill in affirming personal autonomy. No wonder that intuitions conflict in moral philosophy. No wonder people feel confused" (Pence 251). Given the axiological diversity of the contemporary world, how can casuistry hope to operate within it? In a rigorous critique of Jonsen and Toulmin's *Abuse of Casuistry*, Jesuit ethicist Kevin Wildes argues that this diversity is fatal for any modern casuistry. Without a shared background, even the basic narrative of a particular case—let alone a taxonomy of cases—becomes impossible: "Think, for example, of cases about treatment at the end of life. For some the analogous relations of these cases is the intention of the agents, for others the analogous relation is the causal relationship between the physician and the death of the patient, while still others would focus on the exercise of the patients' rights" (*Moral* 112–13). Resolving such differences through casuistry would require a "common justificatory framework" (117) that is unavailable in the modern world. For another version of this argument, see MacIntyre's "Does Applied Ethics Rest on a Mistake?" See also Wildes's "The Priesthood of Bioethics and the Return of Casu-

istry." For a response to Wildes's article, see Tallmon's "How Jonsen Really Views Casuistry"; for Wildes's response, see "Respondeo." For the possibility of a pluralistic casuistry in medical ethics, see Brody (*Life, Taking Issue*). See also Cherry and Iltis.

15. To Burke and Dewey, these kinds of volumes are just the problem. "Any organized mode of understanding and acting," Burke writes, "offers its own possibilities of laxity. In time, there occurs a proliferation of the habits that take advantage of these opportunities" (*ATH* 27). Thus, we get the elaborate casuistries of the period that preceded Pascal. Dewey also blanches at this proliferation and interprets it as a sign of the rule-bound psychosis: "All systems which have committed themselves to belief in a number of hard and fast rules having their origin in conscience, or in the word of God . . . , always have had to resort to a more and more complicated procedure to cover, if possible, all the cases" (Dewey and Tufts 295). Taking Burke and Dewey together here, we might observe that a proliferation of casuistic laxity suggests a literal demoralization insofar as conventional moral systems are no longer appropriate or useful. Casuistry thus brings us to the point at which a new taxonomic category is needed.

WORKS CITED

Aristotle. *Nicomachean Ethics*. 2nd ed. Trans. Terence Irwin. Indianapolis: Hackett, 1999. Print.

———. *On Rhetoric: A Theory of Civic Discourse*. 2nd ed. Trans. George A. Kennedy. New York: Oxford UP, 2007. Print.

Arras, John D. "Getting Down to Cases: The Revival of Casuistry in Bioethics." *Journal of Medicine and Philosophy* 16.1 (1991): 29–51. Print.

———. "Principles and Particularity: The Role of Cases in Bioethics." *Indiana Law Journal* 69.4 (1994): 983–1014. Print.

Arroyo, Sarah J. "Playing to the Tune of Electracy: From Post-Process to a Pedagogy Otherwise." *JAC* 25.4 (2005): 683–715. Print.

Arthos, John. "Where There Are No Rules or Systems to Guide Us: Argument from Example in a Hermeneutic Rhetoric." *QJS* 89.4 (2003): 320–44. Print.

Atwill, Janet M. *Rhetoric Reclaimed: Aristotle and the Liberal Arts Tradition*. Ithaca: Cornell UP, 1998. Print.

Bartholomae, David. "The Tidy House: Basic Writing in the American Curriculum." *Journal of Basic Writing* 12.1 (1993): 4–21. Print.

Bartholomae, David, and John Schilb. "Reconsiderations: 'Inventing the University' at 25: An Interview with David Bartholomae." *College English* 73.3 (2011): 260–82. Print.

Bedau, Hugo Adam. *Making Mortal Choices: Three Exercises in Moral Casuistry*. New York: Oxford UP, 1997. Print.

Berthoff, Ann E. "Learning the Uses of Chaos." Freedman and Pringle 75–78.

———. *The Making of Meaning: Metaphors, Models, and Maxims for Writing Teachers*. Montclair NJ: Boynton/Cook, 1981. Print.

———. "Rhetoric as Hermeneutic." *CCC* 42.3 (1991): 279–87. Print.

Biesecker, Barbara A. "Coming to Terms with Recent Attempts to Write Women into the History of Rhetoric." *Philosophy and Rhetoric* 25.2 (1992): 140–61. Print.

———. "Rethinking the Rhetorical Situation from within the Thematic of *Différance*." *Philosophy and Rhetoric* 22.2 (1989): 110–30. Print.

Bitzer, Lloyd. "The Rhetorical Situation." *Philosophy and Rhetoric* 1.1 (1968): 1–14. Print.

Bizzell, Patricia, and Bruce Herzberg. *The Rhetorical Tradition: Readings from Classical Times to the Present.* Boston: Bedford/St. Martin's, 2001. Print.

Bloom, Lynn Z. "The Great Paradigm Shift and Its Legacy for the Twenty-First Century." *Composition Studies in the New Millennium: Rereading the Past, Rewriting the Future.* Ed. Lynn Z. Bloom, Donald A. Daiker, and Edward M. White. Carbondale: Southern Illinois UP, 2003. 31–47. Print.

Booth, Wayne C. *The Company We Keep: An Ethics of Fiction.* Berkeley: U of California P, 1988. Print.

———. "The Ethics of Teaching Literature." *College English* 61.1 (1998): 41–55. Print.

Booth, Wayne C., and Peter Elbow. "Symposium: The Limits and Alternatives to Skepticism: A Dialogue." *College English* 67.4 (2005): 378–99. Print.

Breuch, Lee-Ann M. Kastman. "Post-Process 'Pedagogy': A Philosophical Exercise." *JAC* 22.1 (2002): 119–50. Print.

Brody, Baruch A. *Life and Death Decision Making.* New York: Oxford UP, 1988. Print.

———. *Taking Issue: Pluralism and Casuistry in Bioethics.* Washington, DC: Georgetown UP, 2004. Print.

Brooke, Collin, and Thomas Rickert. "Being Delicious: Materialities of Rhetoric in a Web 2.0 Application." Dobrin, Rice, and Vastola 163–82.

Burke, Kenneth. *Attitudes toward History.* 3rd ed. Berkeley: U of California P, 1984. Print.

———. *Counter-Statement.* 2nd ed. Berkeley: U of California P, 1968. Print.

———. "Definition of Man." *Language as Symbolic Action: Essays on Life, Literature, and Method.* Berkeley: U of California P, 1966. 3–24. Print.

———. *A Grammar of Motives.* 1945. Berkeley: U of California P, 1969. Print.

———. *Permanence and Change: An Anatomy of Purpose.* 2nd ed. Berkeley: U of California P, 1954. Print.

———. *A Rhetoric of Motives.* Berkeley: U of California P, 1969. Print.

Callon, Michel, Pierre Lascoumes, and Yannick Barthe. *Acting in an Uncertain World: An Essay on Technical Democracy*. Trans. Graham Burchell. Cambridge: MIT P, 2009. Print.

Cherry, Mark J., and Ana Smith Iltis, eds. *Pluralistic Casuistry: Balancing Moral Arguments, Economic Realities, and Political Theory*. Dordrecht, The Netherlands: Springer, 2007. Print.

Cicero, Marcus Tullius. *On Duties*. Ed. M. T. Griffin and E. M. Atkins. Cambridge, UK: Cambridge UP, 1991. Print.

Clifford, John, and Elizabeth Ervin. "The Ethics of Process." Kent, *Post-Process Theory* 179–97.

Consigny, Scott. "Rhetoric and its Situations." *Philosophy and Rhetoric* 7.3 (1974): 175–86. Print.

Cooper, Marilyn M. "The Ecology of Writing." *Writing as Social Action*. Marilyn M. Cooper and Michael Holzman. Portsmouth, NH: Heinemann, 1989. 1–13. Print.

Couture, Barbara. "Modeling and Emulating: Rethinking Agency in the Writing Process." Kent, *Post-Process Theory* 30–48.

Crick, Nathan. "Composition as Experience: John Dewey on Creative Expression and the Origins of 'Mind.'" *CCC* 55.2 (2003): 254–75. Print.

———. *Democracy and Rhetoric: John Dewey on the Arts of Becoming*. Columbia: U of South Carolina P, 2010. Print.

Crowley, Sharon. *Composition in the University: Historical and Polemical Essays*. Pittsburgh: U of Pittsburgh P, 1998. Print.

Davis, D. Diane. *Breaking Up [at] Totality: A Rhetoric of Laughter*. Carbondale: Southern Illinois UP, 2000. Print.

Dawkins, Richard. "If I Ruled the World: Richard Dawkins." *Prospect Magazine* 23 Feb. 2011. Web. 1 July 2012.

Dewey, John. *Art as Experience*. New York: Perigee, 2005. Print.

———. *Democracy and Education: An Introduction to the Philosophy of Education*. New York: Free Press, 1997. Print.

———. *Experience and Education*. New York: Simon, 1997. Print.

———. *Experience and Nature*. Paperback. Mineola, NY: Dover, 2001. Print.

———. "From Absolutism to Experimentalism." *The Later Works of John Dewey, 1925–1953*. Ed. Jo Ann Boydston. Vol. 5. Carbondale: Southern Illinois UP, 1984. 147–60. Print.

———. *How We Think*. Mineola, NY: Dover, 1997. Print.

———. Introduction. *The Use of Resources in Education*. By Elsie Ripley Clapp. New York: Harper, 1952. vii–xi. Print.

————. *The Later Works of John Dewey, 1925–1953: The Quest for Certainty.* Ed. Jo Ann Boydston. Vol. 4. Carbondale: Southern Illinois UP, 2008. Print.

————. *Liberalism and Social Action.* New York: Capricorn, 1963. Print.

————. *Logic: The Theory of Inquiry.* New York: Holt, 1938. Print.

————. "My Pedagogic Creed." *John Dewey on Education: Selected Writings.* Ed. Reginald D. Archambault. Chicago: U of Chicago P, 1974. 427–39. Print.

————. "The Reflex Arc Concept in Psychology." *The Early Works of John Dewey, 1882–1898.* Ed. Jo Ann Boydston. Vol. 5. Carbondale: Southern Illinois UP, 1972. 96–112. Print.

————. *"The School and Society" and "The Child and the Curriculum."* Ed. Philip W. Jackson. Chicago: U of Chicago P, 1990. Print.

Dewey, John, and Arthur F. Bentley. *Knowing and the Known.* Boston: Beacon, 1949. Print.

Dewey, John, and James Tufts. *The Middle Works of John Dewey: Ethics, 1899–1924.* Ed. Jo Ann Boydston. Vol. 5. Carbondale: Southern Illinois UP, 1978. Print.

Dobrin, Sidney I. *Constructing Knowledges: The Politics of Theory-Building and Pedagogy in Composition.* Albany: State U of New York P, 1997. Print.

————. "Paralogic Hermeneutic Theories, Power, and the Possibility for Liberating Pedagogies." Kent, *Post-Process Theory* 132–48.

————. *Postcomposition.* Carbondale: Southern Illinois UP, 2011. Print.

Dobrin, Sidney I., J. A. Rice, and Michael Vastola, eds. *Beyond Postprocess.* Logan: Utah State UP, 2011. Print.

Eagleton, Terry. *After Theory.* New York: Basic Books, 2003.

Edbauer, Jenny. "Unframing Models of Public Distribution: From Rhetorical Situation to Rhetorical Ecologies." *Rhetoric Society Quarterly* 35.4 (2005): 5–24. Print.

Elbow, Peter H. "The Definition of Teaching." *College English* 30.3 (1968): 187–201. Print.

Eldridge, Michael. *Transforming Experience: John Dewey's Cultural Instrumentalism.* Nashville: Vanderbilt UP, 1998. Print.

Emig, Janet. "The Tacit Tradition: The Inevitability of a Multi-Disciplinary Approach to Writing Research." *The Web of Meaning: Essays on Writing, Teaching, Learning, and Thinking.* Ed. Dixie Goswami and Maureen Butler. Upper Montclair, NJ: Boynton/Cook, 1983. 145–56. Print.

Fish, Stanley. "Anti-Foundationalism, Theory Hope, and the Teaching of Composition." *Doing What Comes Naturally: Change, Rhetoric, and the*

Practice of Theory in Literary and Legal Studies. Durham: Duke UP,
1999. 342–55. Print.

———. *The Trouble with Principle.* Cambridge: Harvard UP, 2001. Print.

Fishman, Stephen M., "Explicating Our Tacit Tradition: John Dewey and
Composition Studies." *CCC* 44.3 (1993): 315–30. Print.

Fishman, Stephen M., and Lucille McCarthy. *John Dewey and the Challenge of Classroom Practice.* New York: Teachers College P; Urbana:
NCTE, 1998. Print.

Fishman, Stephen M., and Lucille Parkinson McCarthy. "Teaching for
Student Change: A Deweyan Alternative to Radical Pedagogy." *CCC*
47.3 (1996): 342–66. Print.

Freedman, Aviva, and Ian Pringle. *Reinventing the Rhetorical Tradition.*
Conway, AR: L & S Books, 1980. Print.

Fulkerson, Richard. "The Epistemic Paradoxes of 'Lore': From *The Making of Knowledge in Composition* to the Present (Almost)." *The Changing of Knowledge in Composition: Contemporary Perspectives.* Ed. Lance
Massey and Richard C. Gebhardt. Logan: Utah State UP, 2011. 47–
62. Print.

———. "Of Pre- and Post-Process: Review and Ruminations." *Composition Studies* 29.2 (2001): 93–119. Print.

Gebhardt, Richard C. "Editor's Column: Diversity in a Mainline Journal." *CCC* 43.1 (1992): 7–10. Print.

Goodrich, Peter. "The New Casuistry." *Critical Inquiry* 33 (2007): 673–
709. Print.

Graff, Gerald. *Clueless in Academe: How Schooling Obscures the Life of the
Mind.* New Haven: Yale UP, 2003. Print.

Gutiérrez, Gustavo. *A Theology of Liberation.* Rev. ed. Trans. and ed. Sister
Caridad Inda and John Eagleson. Maryknoll, NY: Orbis, 1988. Print.

Harkin, Patricia. "The Postdisciplinary Politics of Lore." Harkin and
Schilb 124–138.

Harkin, Patricia, and John Schilb. *Contending with Words: Composition
and Rhetoric in a Postmodern Age.* New York: MLA, 1991. Print.

Harris, Joseph. *A Teaching Subject: Composition since 1966.* Upper Saddle
River, NJ: Prentice Hall, 1997. Print.

Hawhee, Debra. *Bodily Arts: Rhetoric and Athletics in Ancient Greece.* Aus-
tin: U of Texas P, 2004. Print.

Hawk, Byron. *A Counter-History of Composition: Toward Methodologies of
Complexity.* Pittsburgh: U of Pittsburgh P, 2007. Print.

———. "Toward a Post-*Techne*—Or, Inventing Pedagogies for Professional Writing." *TCQ* 13.4 (2004): 371–92. Print.

Haynes, Cynthia. "Writing Offshore: The Disappearing Coastline of Composition Theory." *JAC* 23.4 (2003): 667–724. Print.

Hildebrand, David. *Dewey: A Beginner's Guide.* Oxford: Oneworld, 2008. Print.

Hofstadter, Richard. *Anti-Intellectualism in American Life.* New York: Vintage, 1963. Print.

Horton, Myles, and Paulo Freire. *We Make the Road by Walking: Conversations on Education and Social Change.* Philadelphia: Temple UP, 1990. Print.

Jarratt, Susan C. *Rereading the Sophists: Classical Rhetoric Refigured.* Carbondale: Southern Illinois UP, 1991. Print.

Jones, Donald C. "Beyond the Postmodern Impasse of Agency: The Resounding Relevance of John Dewey's Tacit Tradition." *JAC* 16.1 (1996): 81–102. Print.

———. "John Dewey and Peter Elbow: A Pragmatist Revision of Social Theory and Practice." *Rhetoric Review* 21.3 (2002): 264–81. Print.

Jonsen, Albert R. "Casuistry: An Alternative or Complement to Principles?" *Kennedy Institute of Ethics Journal* 5.3 (1995): 237–51. Print.

——— "Casuistry as Methodology in Clinical Ethics." *Theoretical Medicine and Bioethics* 12.4 (1991): 295–307. Print.

———. "Of Balloons and Bicycles; or, the Relationship between Ethical Theory and Practical Judgment." *Hastings Center Report* 21.5 (1991): 14–16. Print.

———. "Platonic Insults: Casuistical." *Common Knowledge* 2.2 (1993): 48–66. Print.

Jonsen, Albert R., and Stephen Toulmin. *The Abuse of Casuistry: A History of Moral Reasoning.* Berkeley: U of California P, 1989. Print.

Kameen, Paul. *Writing/Teaching: Essays toward a Rhetoric of Pedagogy.* Pittsburgh: U of Pittsburgh P, 2000. Print.

Kent, Thomas. "Introduction." Kent, *Post-Process Theory* 1–6.

———. *Paralogic Rhetoric: A Theory of Communicative Interaction.* Cranbury, NJ: Bucknell UP, 1993. Print.

———, ed. *Post-Process Theory: Beyond the Writing-Process Paradigm.* Carbondale: Southern Illinois UP, 1999. Print.

———. "Preface: Righting Writing." Dobrin, Rice, and Vastola xi–xxii.

———. "Principled Pedagogy: A Reply to Lee-Ann M. Kastman Breuch." *JAC* 22.2 (2002): 428–33. Print.

Kirk, Kenneth E. *Conscience and its Problems: An Introduction to Casuistry.* Louisville: Westminster John Knox, 1999. Print.

Kopelman, Loretta M. "Case Method and Casuistry: The Problem of Bias." *Theoretical Medicine and Bioethics* 15.1 (1994): 21–37. Print.

Lanham, Richard. "The Q Question." *The Electronic Word: Democracy, Technology, and the Arts.* Chicago: University of Chicago P, 1993. 154–94. Print.

Latour, Bruno. "Why Has Critique Run out of Steam? From Matters of Fact to Matters of Concern." *Critical Inquiry* 30 (2004): 225–48. Print.

Levi, Edward H. *An Introduction to Legal Reasoning.* Chicago: U of Chicago P, 1962. Print.

Lindemann, Erika. *A Rhetoric for Writing Teachers.* 4th ed. New York: Oxford UP, 2001. Print.

Lyotard, Jean-François. *The Postmodern Condition: a Report on Knowledge.* Minneapolis: U of Minnesota P, 1984. Print.

Lyotard, Jean-François, and Jean-Loup Thébaud. *Just Gaming.* Minneapolis: U of Minnesota P, 1985. Print.

Machado, Antonio. *Selected Poems of Antonio Machado.* Baton Rouge: Louisiana State UP, 1978. Print.

MacIntyre, Alasdair. *After Virtue: A Study in Moral Theory.* 2nd ed. Notre Dame: U of Notre Dame P, 1984. Print.

———. "Does Applied Ethics Rest on a Mistake?" *The Monist* 67.4 (1964): 498–513. Print.

Maryks, Robert Alexsander. *Saint Cicero and the Jesuits: The Influence of the Liberal Arts on the Adoption of Moral Probabilism.* Aldershot, UK: Ashgate, 2008. Print.

Matsuda, Paul Kei. "Process and Post-Process: A Discursive History." *Journal of Second Language Writing* 12.1 (2003): 65–83. Print.

McComiskey, Bruce. "The Post-Process Movement in Composition Studies." *Reforming College Composition: Writing the Wrongs.* Ed. Ray Wallace, Alan Jackson, and Susan Lewis Wallace. Westport, CT: Greenwood, 2000. 37–54. Print.

McKee, Heidi, and James E. Porter. "The Ethics of Digital Writing Research: A Rhetorical Approach." *CCC* 59.4 (2008): 711–49. Print.

McLaughlin, Grace. "An Experiment in Translating Experience into Abstraction." *CCC* 21.3 (1970): 269–71. Print.

Menand, Louis. *The Metaphysical Club.* New York: Farrar, 2002. Print.

Mendelson, Michael. *Many Sides: A Protagorean Approach to the Theory, Practice, and Pedagogy of Argument.* Boston: Kluwer, 2002. Print.

Miller, Richard B. *Casuistry and Modern Ethics: A Poetics of Practical Reasoning.* Chicago: U of Chicago P, 1996. Print.

Miller, Richard E. "The Coming Apocalypse." *Pedagogy* 10.1 (2010): 143–151. Print.

———. *Writing at the End of the World.* Pittsburgh: U of Pittsburgh P, 2005. Print.

Mouffe, Chantal. *The Democratic Paradox.* London: Verso, 2000. Print.

Muckelbauer, John. *The Future of Invention: Rhetoric, Postmodernism, and the Problem of Change.* Albany: State U of New York P, 2008. Print

Newkirk, Thomas. *More Than Stories: The Range of Children's Writing.* Portsmouth, NH: Heinemann, 1989. Print.

Nietzsche, Friedrich. *The Portable Nietzsche.* Ed. and trans. Walter Arnold Kaufmann. New York: Penguin, 1976. Print.

North, Stephen M. *The Making of Knowledge in Composition: Portrait of an Emerging Field.* Upper Montclair, N.J.: Boynton/Cook, 1987. Print.

Nussbaum, Martha Craven. *The Fragility of Goodness: Luck and Ethics in Greek Tragedy and Philosophy.* Cambridge, UK: Cambridge UP, 1986. Print.

Ohmann, Richard. *English in America: A Radical View of the Profession.* Middletown, CT: Wesleyan UP; Hanover, NH: UP of New England, 1996. Print.

Olson, Gary A. "The Death of Composition as an Intellectual Discipline." *Rhetoric and Composition as Intellectual Work.* Ed. Gary A. Olson. Carbondale: Southern Illinois UP, 2002. 23–31. Print.

———. "Toward a Post-Process Composition: Abandoning the Rhetoric of Assertion." Kent, *Post-Process Theory* 7–15.

———. "Why Distrust the Very Goals with Which You Began?" *JAC* 22.2 (2002): 423–28. Print.

O'Malley, John W. *The First Jesuits.* Cambridge: Harvard UP, 1993. Print.

Ong, Walter J. *Ramus, Method, and the Decay of Dialogue: From the Art of Discourse to the Art of Reason.* Chicago: U of Chicago P, 2004. Print.

Pascal, Blaise. *"Pensées":"The Provincial Letters."* New York: Random, 1941. Print.

Peach, Lucinda Joy. "Feminist Cautions about Casuistry: The Supreme Court's Abortion Decisions as Paradigms." *Policy Studies* 27.2/3 (1994): 143–60. Print.

Pence, Greg. "Virtue Theory." *A Companion to Ethics.* Ed. Peter Singer. Cambridge: Blackwell, 1991. 248–58. Print.

Pender, Kelly. "Negation and the Contradictory Technics of Rhetoric." *RSQ* 38.1 (2008): 2–24. Print.

———. *Techne, from Neoclassicism to Postmodernism: Understanding Writing as a Useful, Teachable Art.* Anderson, SC: Parlor, 2011. Print.

Petraglia, Joseph. "Is There Life After Process? The Role of Social Scientism in a Changing Discipline." Kent, *Post-Process Theory* 49–64.

Phelps, Louise Wetherbee. *Composition as a Human Science: Contributions to the Self-Understanding of a Discipline.* New York: Oxford UP, 1991. Print.

Pope, Alexander. "The Rape of the Lock." *Norton Anthology of English Literature.* 5th ed. Vol. 1. New York: Norton, 1986. 2233–51. Print.

Quintilian. *The Institutio Oratoria of Quintilian.* Trans. H. E. Butler. 4 vols. Cambridge: Harvard UP, 1961. Print.

Ratcliffe, Krista. *Rhetorical Listening: Identification, Gender, Whiteness.* Carbondale: Southern Illinois UP, 2005. Print.

The Ratio Studiorum: The Official Plan for Jesuit Education. Trans. Claude Pavur. St. Louis: Institute of Jesuit Sources, 2005. Print.

Rickert, Thomas. *Acts of Enjoyment: Rhetoric, Žižek, and the Return of the Subject.* Pittsburgh: U of Pittsburgh P, 2007. Print.

———. "Toward the *Chora*: Kristeva, Derrida, and Ulmer on Emplaced Invention." *Philosophy and Rhetoric* 40.3 (2007): 251–73. Print.

Roskelly, Hephzibah, and Kate Ronald. *Reason to Believe: Romanticism, Pragmatism, and the Teaching of Writing.* Albany: State U of New York P, 1998. Print.

Russell, David. "Activity Theory and Process Approaches: Writing (Power) in School and Society." Kent, *Post-Process Theory* 80–95.

———. "Vygotsky, Dewey, and Externalism: Beyond the Student/Discipline Dichotomy." *JAC* 13.1 (1993): 173–97. Print.

Sampson, Margaret. "Laxity and Liberty in Seventeenth-Century English Political Thought." *Conscience and Casuistry in Early Modern Europe.* Ed. Edmund Leites. New York: Cambridge UP, 1988. 72–118. Print.

Sánchez, Raúl. "First, a Word." Dobrin, Rice, and Vastola. 183–194. Print.

———. *The Function of Theory in Composition Studies.* Albany: State U of New York P, 2005. Print.

Sandel, Michael J. *Justice: What's the Right Thing to Do?* New York: Farrar, 2009. Print.

Schön, Donald A. *Educating the Reflective Practitioner: Toward a New Design for Teaching and Learning in the Professions.* San Francisco: Jossey-Bass, 1987. Print.

———. *The Reflective Practitioner: How Professionals Think in Action.* New York: Basic, 1983. Print.

Schwartz, Barry, and Kenneth E. Sharpe. "Practical Wisdom: Aristotle Meets Positive Psychology." *Journal of Happiness Studies* 7.3 (2006): 377–95. Print.

———. *Practical Wisdom: The Right Way to Do the Right Thing.* New York: Riverhead, 2010. Print.

Schilb, John. "Editor's Note." *College English* 74.6 (2012): 513–19. Print.

Strong, Carson. "Justification in Ethics." *Moral Theory and Moral Judgments in Medical Ethics*. Ed. Baruch A. Brody. Boston: Kluwer, 1988. 193–212. Print.

Sunstein, Cass R. *Legal Reasoning and Political Conflict*. New York: Oxford UP, 1998. Print.

Tallmon, James M. "Casuistry." Ed. Thomas O. Sloane. *Encyclopedia of Rhetoric*. New York: Oxford UP, 2001. 83–88. Print.

———. "Casuistry and the Role of Rhetorical Reason in Ethical Inquiry." *Philosophy and Rhetoric* 28.4 (1995): 377–87. Print.

———. "How Jonsen Really Views Casuistry: A Note on the Abuse of Father Wildes." *Journal of Medicine and Philosophy* 19.1 (1994): 103–13. Print.

Taylor, Charles. "The Rushdie Controversy." *Public Culture* 2.1 (1989): 118–22. Print.

Taylor, Mark C. *The Moment of Complexity: Emerging Network Culture*. Chicago: U of Chicago P, 2002. Print.

Tomlinson, Tom. "Casuistry in Medical Ethics: Rehabilitated, or Repeat Offender?" *Theoretical Medicine* 15 (1994): 5–20. Print.

Toner, Lisa Marie. "Ethical Roles for the Writing Teacher: A Rhetorical Casuistic Perspective." Diss. Purdue U, 1996. Print.

Toulmin, Stephen. *Cosmopolis: The Hidden Agenda of Modernity*. Chicago: U of Chicago P, 1992. Print.

———. "The National Commission on Human Experimentation: Procedures and Outcomes." *Scientific Controversies: Case Studies in the Resolution and Closure of Disputes in Science and Technology*. Ed. H. Tristram Engelhardt Jr. and Arthur L. Caplan. New York: Cambridge UP, 1987. 599–614. Print.

———. "The Tyranny of Principles." *Hastings Center Report* 11.6 (1981): 31–39. Print.

Vatz, Richard E. "The Myth of the Rhetorical Situation." *Philosophy and Rhetoric* 6.3 (1973): 154–61. Print.

Vitanza, Victor J. "Concerning a Postclassical Ethos as Para/Rhetorical Ethics, the 'Selphs,' and the Excluded Third." *Ethos: New Essays in Rhetorical and Critical Theory*. Ed. James Baumlin and Tita French Baumlin. Dallas: Southern Methodist UP, 1994. 389–431. Print.

———. "Critical Sub/Versions in the History of Philosophical Rhetoric." *Rhetoric Review* 6.1 (1987): 41–66. Print.

———. *Negation, Subjectivity, and the History of Rhetoric*. Albany: State U of New York P, 1997. Print.

———. "'Some More' Notes, toward a 'Third' Sophistic." *Argumentation* 5.2 (1991): 117–39. Print.

———. "Three Countertheses: Or, A Critical In(ter)vention into Composition Theories and Pedagogies." Harkin and Schilb 139–72.

Voss, Ralph F., and Michael L. Keene. "Against the Wind: Teaching Composition in the 'Post-process' Era." *Against the Grain: A Volume in Honor of Maxine Hairston.* Ed. David Joliffe, et al. Cresskill, NJ: Hampton, 2002. 249–77. Print.

Westbrook, Robert B. *John Dewey and American Democracy.* Ithaca: Cornell UP, 1991. Print.

White, Eric Charles. *Kaironomia: On the Will-to-Invent.* Ithaca: Cornell UP, 1987. Print.

Wilde, Oscar. "The Soul of Man under Socialism." *The Artist as Critic: Critical Writings of Oscar Wilde.* Ed. Richard Ellmann. Chicago: U of Chicago P, 1982. 255–89. Print.

Wildes, Kevin Wm. *Moral Acquaintances: Methodology in Bioethics.* Notre Dame: U of Notre Dame P, 2000. Print.

———. "The Priesthood of Bioethics and the Return of Casuistry." *Journal of Medicine and Philosophy.* 18.1 (1993): 33–49. Print.

———. "Respondeo: Method and Content in Casuistry." *Journal of Medicine and Philosophy.* 19.1 (1994): 115–19. Print.

Worsham, Lynn. "Writing Against Writing: The Predicament of Écriture *Féminine* in Composition Studies." Harkin and Schilb, 82–104.

Wright, Jaime. "Argument in Holocaust Denial: The Differences between Historical Casuistry and Denial Casuistry." *Argumentation and Advocacy* 43.2 (2006): 51–64. Print.

Wysocki, Anne Frances. "It Is Not Only Ours." *CCC* 59.2 (2007): 282–88. Print.

Yarbrough, Stephen R. *After Rhetoric: The Study of Discourse beyond Language and Culture.* Carbondale: Southern Illinois UP, 1999.

Young, Richard. "Arts, Crafts, Gifts, and Knacks: Some Disharmonies in New Rhetoric." Freedman and Pringle 53–61.

INDEX

AUTHOR

 **Paul Lynch** is assistant professor of English at Saint Louis University, where he teaches courses in rhetoric and composition. His work has appeared in *College Composition and Communication, College English, Pedagogy, Present Tense,* and *Rhetoric Review.*

OTHER BOOKS IN THE CCCC STUDIES IN WRITING & RHETORIC SERIES

This book was typeset in Garamond and Frutiger by Barbara Frazier. Typefaces used on the cover include Adobe Garamond and Formata. The book was printed on 55-lb. Natural Offset paper by Victor Graphics, Inc.